Praise for

IT WAS AN UGLY COUCH ANYWAY

"Elizabeth's wit and writing style are as pure as they are delightful. Readers can expect to feel as if they're on a rainy-day cafe date with a best friend and will enjoy this honest, funny, and candid trip through stories of a life lived one unpredictable but silver-lined day at a time."

—BUNMI LADITAN, AUTHOR OF *THE HONEST TODDLER*,
DEAR GOD, AND *HELP ME, GOD, I'M A PARENT*

"*It Was an Ugly Couch Anyway* is a delight—wise, funny, beautifully written. I devoured it in a day. And cried a little, for a couch I never sat on. I loved this book."

—JULIA CLAIBORNE JOHNSON, AUTHOR OF *BE FRANK
WITH ME* AND *BETTER LUCK NEXT TIME*

"I love reading anything Elizabeth writes because, well, she's hilarious, and I really admire that in a person. But there's another aspect of Elizabeth's writing that's on fine display in *It Was An Ugly Couch Anyway*: a grounded, sincere tenderness that anchors every bit of her humor. Whether she's writing about marriage, health, faith, work, or a complicated real estate transaction (I don't mean to be dramatic, but I experienced secondary stress), Elizabeth opens the door to her very real life and rolls out the proverbial welcome mat as she shares her stories. The end result is a book with so much heart that it's going to feel like home to the people who are lucky enough to read it. What an absolute gift."

—SOPHIE HUDSON, BESTSELLING AUTHOR
AND CO-HOST OF *THE BIG BOO CAST*

"It's rare to find a book that's illuminating and very funny, but this essay collection is both. Crack it open for a deep dive into the insanity of Manhattan real estate, and stay for Elizabeth's clear-eyed and deeply humane insight into modern life in all of its complexities."

—SHANNON REED, AUTHOR OF *WHY DID I GET A B?*

"A buffet of honesty, humor, and quirkiness that borders on chaos, Elizabeth Passarella's writing gives us permission to cherish the strange experiences and honest mistakes that make us human. This book is a heckuva ride and I devoured every word."

—SHANNAN MARTIN, AUTHOR OF *START WITH HELLO* AND *THE MINISTRY OF ORDINARY PLACES*

"Elizabeth Passarella's collection of essays is a delightful mix of contradictions, like the author herself: a devout Christian with an unholy real estate obsession; a devoted mother who can't wait for her alone time; a journalist who walked away from a job at a big-time media company; a native Southerner who has wholeheartedly adopted the most liberal corner of New York City as her own. But above all, Passarella's memoir is about a woman's fierce determination to find a home for her family (and at a good price too), without losing her humanity, in the building she loves. As her neighbor, I was rooting for her all the way."

—PAULA DERROW, EDITOR OF *BEHIND THE BEDROOM DOOR*

IT WAS AN UGLY COUCH ANYWAY

IT WAS AN UGLY COUCH ANYWAY

and other thoughts on moving forward

ELIZABETH PASSARELLA

NELSON BOOKS

An Imprint of Thomas Nelson

Published in Nashville, Tennessee, by Nelson Books, an imprint of Thomas Nelson. Nelson Books and Thomas Nelson are registered trademarks of HarperCollins Christian Publishing, Inc.

Thomas Nelson titles may be purchased in bulk for educational, business, fund-raising, or sales promotional use. For information, please email SpecialMarkets@ThomasNelson.com.

Scripture quotations are taken from The Holy Bible, New International Version®, NIV®. Copyright © 1973, 1978, 1984, 2011 by Biblica, Inc.® Used by permission of Zondervan. All rights reserved worldwide. www.Zondervan.com. The "NIV" and "New International Version" are trademarks registered in the United States Patent and Trademark Office by Biblica, Inc.®

Any internet addresses, phone numbers, or company or product information printed in this book are offered as a resource and are not intended in any way to be or to imply an endorsement by Thomas Nelson, nor does Thomas Nelson vouch for the existence, content, or services of these sites, phone numbers, companies, or products beyond the life of this book.

Some names and identifying factors have been changed to protect the privacy of others.

ISBN 978-1-4002-1901-8 (TP)
ISBN 978-1-4002-1903-2 (eBook)

Library of Congress Control Number 2022047478

Printed in the United States of America
23 24 25 26 27 LBC 5 4 3 2 1

for my neighbors

Sadness is like a little bit of an emotional death, but not a defeat if you can find a way to laugh about it.

—*Stephen Colbert*

I say too many words to be right a lot.

—*Beth Moore*

Contents

CONTENTS

Prologue

HOME

I'M BEING A LITTLE BIT OF A COWARD ABOUT GETTING MY SECOND tattoo, even though going ahead and just *doing it* would make finishing this book a whole lot easier.

I'm writing this part last. After everything that has happened. Now that I know how it all ends.

I used to think I wanted this tattoo to signify my kids—the three I have and the two I miscarried. I've written about it before, almost as if I were trying to hold myself to it. And then a couple of years passed, and I hadn't managed to come up with anything. No symbol or drawing or phrase felt right to me. It is hard to encapsulate multiple children or the breadth of motherhood in one discreet mark, I told myself. Or maybe being a mother wasn't the identity I wanted to celebrate, indelibly, on my body anymore. That thought crossed my mind.

By contrast, deciding on my first tattoo was easy. I was twenty, studying abroad in London, and wanted a Jesus fish on my foot. I liked Jesus then. I still like him; I've never regretted the tattoo.

PROLOGUE

There was a flat of boys living above me who were part of the same study-abroad program, and one of them, Stefan, said he knew of a tattoo shop in Central London and would take me. Shortly before our appointment we were all packing up our rooms because our semester was ending, and I went upstairs to find Stefan swallowing the boys' pet goldfish that they'd bought when they moved in. Everyone was leaving the country in a few days, and the boys weren't sure what to do with the fish. Stefan gulped it down like an oyster. This is the man I trusted to find me a tattoo artist.

If I wasn't going to get a second tattoo to honor my children, shouldn't I have just dropped it? Most likely. I am forty-six years old. Not that I believe there is an age cutoff for getting tattoos—absolutely not. The issue was more that I'd lived that long without wanting another one. Why now, in middle age, when I'd been so settled as a one-tattoo person for half my life?

The desire did not go away, though. It kept nagging at me. Some mornings I would roll over to my husband and workshop ideas. "What about your initials? That would be simple. I love you. I could get your initials," I'd say.

"Are we talking about your tattoo again?" he would ask.

"Yes."

"No. Your next husband might not like it."

"That's not funny."

"Yes it is. Get whatever you want."

But I didn't know what I wanted.

And then one day I was running—something I used to loathe but changed my mind about a couple of years ago, a situation I'll explain later on. I took a route I'd taken a hundred times before: out the lobby of our apartment building, down the street a few blocks, into Central Park, south to the Reservoir, around it and over to the East Side, then back to the West Side, and north again toward home. In seasons when I was in better shape, I circled it twice.

I used an app on my phone to track my pace, and at the end of every run, the map of my route popped up. What showed on the screen was a loop with a wiggly tail on top, sort of a roundish Little Dipper or a lasso or a golf driver that had melted in the sun. That day, when the map filled my phone screen for the umpteenth time, I remembered a story I'd read a few years ago on a blog. The story was about quirky tattoos. One woman had copied the outline of a marking on her dog's chest and had it tattooed on her bicep. People never knew what it was; they'd always guess a state (the closest, I thought, was an upside-down Michigan). My tattoo would be similar, the outline of something recognizable only to me. I could imagine people seeing it and coming up with theories, wondering what the story was behind it. Or not seeing it at all, and it would be a story I could keep to myself.

This is the story. This book, in a way. And I regret to inform you of this meandering truth: that I went from wanting a tattoo that displayed a love of my children to wanting a tattoo that displayed a love of my husband to wanting a tattoo that displayed a love of an apartment building. What can I say? Real estate in New York is a very serious thing.

My husband, Michael, and I bought an apartment a couple of years after we got married. We stayed in that apartment for almost fourteen years. All of our children came home from the hospital to that apartment, and we loved it. But more than that, we loved the neighborhood and the park across the street and the people in our building. As homes often are, that two-bedroom apartment was our anchor, our refuge, when circumstances were constantly changing. We sold the apartment in 2021, and this story I'm telling you is about our half-crazy attempt to stay in the building by purchasing a different, larger apartment on another floor. It involves the widow of the owner—who became my constant phone companion, a massive (gigantic!) hoarding situation, one Christmas card featuring chipmunks wearing tutus, and some medical machinery from the 1950s that I gave away and am now convinced was worth a fortune. Probably not, but I still lose sleep.

While we were in the middle of the saga, on days when Michael and I worried that our dream of staying in the building and buying this much-bigger apartment was never going to come to fruition, I would mention getting my new tattoo. It became my talisman, this path from our home, through my favorite route in the park, and back to our home. Our home we wanted to live in forever, if we could just get some paperwork moving. Michael kept telling me to wait. "You cannot get that tattoo unless we actually own the apartment," he said. What if we didn't get it? What if we moved downtown and I had this dumb outline of a map to and from our old place? What if it made me sad for the rest of my life? He was right. I listened, and I did not get the tattoo. But I know why I wanted it so badly. It was something permanent, tying me to a place that I loved in a tumultuous year. And yes, there was a bit of magical thinking that finally taking the plunge would shift the winds in our favor, as embarrassing as that is to admit.

This is a book about moving, which, in general, I hate. See: fighting tooth and nail to stay in the same building rather than having to acclimate to a different subway stop. Yes, it is the story of moving out and trying to move back. But it is also about the displacement we often feel, even when our surroundings haven't budged. If the wildness and brokenness of the past few years have taught me anything, it is that whatever you think is solid in this world will shift, and that includes your strongest-held opinions about yourself. I have reassessed my stance on everything from running to dogs to whether it was a good idea for me to have children. (If that seems like an outrageous thing to ponder, you might want to skip chapter 9, where I write about losing my child in the middle of Times Square on Christmas Eve.) I also wrote about my evolving perspective on my mother-in-law, which is most likely an even bigger mistake than admitting you lost a child in Times Square. But moving and unpacking—of all kinds—is messy.

These are stories of what we hold on to, and what we can let go. They are about trudging forward without certainty, without a clear destination. They are about looking back on where we've been and being okay if it's maybe worse, or different, than we remember. Sometimes you move through a difficult month or a medical crisis or even a memory and end up in a fresh place. Other times you circle around a wiggly path that in your running app looks like a latke with a hair trailing from one side and return to where you started—but with newfound peace. I hope these stories remind you, as they have me, that we have less control than we think, that the hard parts don't last forever, and that apartment dreams can come true. You just need a lot of patience and a dumpster.

Chapter 1

IT WAS AN UGLY COUCH ANYWAY

THE FIRST THOUGHT I HAD AFTER MY HUSBAND AND I FINALLY decided it was time to sell our two-bedroom apartment was if there was a proper technique for skinning a couch. I needed to get rid of the couch—our real estate agent had said very plainly that it had to go, the sooner the better—and yet I was very attached to the fabric, for reasons I'll get into shortly. I knew there had to be a way to cut the upholstery in just the right places so that I could strip it off in sheets, like peeling off the back of contact paper.

"You don't need all of it. Keep a small square of the fabric. Frame it, whatever, and move on," said my sister, Holland, when I explained on the phone what I was about to do.

"But I want to save as much of the fabric as I can."

"Why? What do you think you're going to do with it?"

"I don't know. Seat cushions. A headboard. So I can keep a memory of him. It's like when people taxidermy their dead dogs.

You know people do that, right? They use the skin to make, like, a stuffed animal replica that then sits in their living room forever."

"So you are taxidermy-ing our dad?"

I took a drink of my gin and tonic. "Something like that."

My mother was all for it. "Take pictures," she said.

My father bought the couch in question in 1968, three years before he married my mother. He ordered it from some family friends who owned an upscale furniture store in Memphis, and while I guess it's possible that a salesperson talked him into the upholstery, I've always assumed it was his deliberate, well-thought-out choice. This was a man who used to order swatches of knit turtleneck fabric in various jewel tones from L.L.Bean so he could match future turtlenecks to his existing sport coats (a service I'm certain no longer exists at L.L.Bean). His couch design was personal. This thing was nine feet long—long enough for two people to stretch out comfortably, my dad always said—and low to the ground, with narrow, boxy arms that were even with the back of the frame. It was a simple, modern couch. And the fabric was a baby-soft velour plaid in the harmonious shades of rust, darker rust, coralish rust, cream, and black.

Everyone but my dad hated the look of the couch. At least, that's what we all said.

"You're all going to fight over this couch someday," he would tell me and my sister.

"No way. It is sooo ugly, Dad. So ugly. Ew," was our typical response.

It was ugly. But it was comfortable—comfortable in a way that made you see the ugliness differently. Sitting down, you would instantly start petting the velour on the cushion underneath you, absentmindedly running your hands away from the sides of your thighs and bringing them back in, tucking them under your rear end to feel the soft springiness of the cushions. At that point, most people would swing their legs onto the couch ("Wow! You could fit two people end to end on here!") and lie back, still moving arms and legs across the fabric like they were making a snow angel because they simply couldn't stop. I have memories of lying on the couch in the summer with bare legs and feeling the coolness of the velour lower my body temperature. Weirdly, it was also cozy and warm in the winter. And durable! That's the most amazing part. My wedding dress, for which I paid almost $2,000, fell apart— one strap popped loose, and every single covered button fell off the back—in a single evening of dancing. Yet the 1968 velour uphol- stery on my dad's couch looked perfect, even after forty years of bottoms and elbows and drooling faces smushed into it. Perfect.

Once my parents were married and raising children, my mother did not want the rust plaid in her living room, even though she, too, knew it was the most comfortable fabric in the world. So the couch lived for a while at my grandparents' cabin on Lake Mohawk in northern Mississippi. When they sold the cabin, the couch came back to my parents' house in Memphis. It went into my grandmother's bedroom next to the garage. When it became necessary for her nurse, Chris, to occasionally stay overnight, Chris would sleep on the velour couch next to my grandmother's bed. In high school I probably spent more time back in that bedroom watching TV with my grandmother than I might have otherwise, because the couch would suck me in. Perhaps that was part of its magic, holding me there in the final year of my grandmother's life.

When she died, the couch went into the attic, stored on its end like an obelisk to conserve floor space.

In 2004 I moved the couch to New Orleans because Michael and I were engaged, and he was in law school at Tulane, and the apartment that I rented had a living room wall that could handle a nine-foot couch.

"But you'll need to slipcover it," said my mother.

"Of course," I said.

"That's a crime," said my dad.

I bought yards and yards of fabric and hired a seamstress to make a slipcover for the couch. I was going to hide its velour-plaid glory under a respectable, chocolate-brown velvet. When the seamstress arrived at my apartment to deliver the slipcover, I could immediately tell it wasn't going to work. She'd taken measurements. The sewing was beautiful. But as she began to drape and tuck the new fabric around the old couch, nothing quite fit. When we would pull one end over an arm or tuck it along a seam, the other side would come loose. The cushions didn't fill out the pillowcases. It was as if the couch was simultaneously recoiling from and regurgitating a vegetable it didn't care for. We'd have friends over, and once people got up from sitting on the couch, the brown would be shifted aside and the plaid velour would be peeking through, like a negligee. I would spend half an hour every day redraping and tucking to make the couch look decent. After graduation, when Michael and I moved back to New York City, I folded up the slip-cover and left it in my parents' garage. The couch was free.

My parents encouraged my new husband and me to take the couch back to New York. In their minds it was being rehomed to a better place, a city where furniture born in the South that no longer felt like it fit in the South (meaning it was not in the English country style that my mother now embraced) could be welcomed for its boldness and finally be happy. They could have also been talking about their daughter, for what it's worth. Michael was taking both of us, me and the couch, off of their hands, and everyone was thrilled.

The only problem was that a nine-foot couch needs room to breathe. Michael and I were moving into an apartment that was the biggest I'd ever lived in—my previous New York City couch was a loveseat that pulled out into a twin bed. Still the plaid couch was too big for our living room. We stored it in my in-laws' garage in Connecticut and bought a normal-sized couch. I would forget about my dad's couch until he'd ask about it on a phone call, like a parent checking on a kid at college. Was it protected from water damage? Were all the cushions intact? It surely was a shame I wasn't using it, he would say. It was such a comfortable couch.

I tried to forget about it. I knew it wasn't totally protected in the garage. I knew it was getting dusty and banged up and had a large black stain from something greasy that rubbed against it in the moving truck from New Orleans. I knew my dad would be disappointed in how I was caring for the couch, so I put it out of my mind and figured I'd toss it when he died. Then my in-laws sold their house and said, "We're giving the couch to the gardener if you don't come get it."

That's how the couch ended up in my children's bedroom. In our two-bedroom apartment, which we bought three years after we got married, Michael and I sleep in the smaller bedroom and the kids have the master. It's a large room that fits their bunk beds with plenty of space left over for toys and bookshelves. It has a very long wall that, with a little rearranging, fit my dad's couch, which arrived looking tired and grungy and dull. I felt terrible. I gently vacuumed the cushions and in the corners of the frame. I rinsed and dabbed at different stains like I was cleaning wounds. I grimaced at the threads that were pulling in certain places, wondering how long we had until the fabric sprouted holes. But then I lay down and swept my arms back and forth. It was just as soft, just as silky and cool. This past summer we visited friends who were babysitting rabbits that had been rescued from the show circuit. I can't say for sure what qualifies a rabbit as a show rabbit or why they needed to be rescued—although these guys did have ID numbers tattooed on the insides of their ears—but they were the softest rabbits I have ever felt. It was like running my hand over a sea of baby eyelashes. The couch still felt just like that, after all those years.

My dad was thrilled to have it back in action. In the last five or six years of his life, he got to visit his couch quite a bit. Whenever my parents came to New York, they stayed with us, and the sleeping arrangements were as follows: Michael and I remained in our queen-sized bed, my mother slept with my middle child on the bottom, full-sized bunk, and my dad slept on the couch. His couch. Whenever I would plead with him and my mom to take our bed, he would say, "Are you kidding? That couch is the most comfortable bed in the house." He greeted it with quiet reverence every time he visited, even after the fabric began to split and the frame bowed in the front—a result of my three kids using the couch as an urban trampoline. I wonder if he would have told me to get rid of it or been disappointed that I did. I'm glad I never had to find out. He died in 2019, around the time that the original metal springs began popping through the seat, pushing fifty-year-old cotton batting and foam onto the bedroom floor in chunks.

When loved ones die, we become suddenly, desperately attached to material things we never knew we cared about. The Bible says, "Do not store up for yourselves treasures on earth, where moths and vermin destroy, and where thieves break in and steal" (Matthew 6:19), and I'd add, "and where your formerly unsentimental children become so emotional about inanimate objects you loved that they find themselves skinning a couch while weeping uncontrollably." A few months ago, my husband found a dress shirt that my dad had left hanging in our closet on his last visit and asked if he could donate it. I said yes, but only after my husband added, kindly, "It doesn't smell like him, just so you know. I think it's been dry-cleaned."

My mother is hoarding his last bottle of cologne, and I've seriously considered ordering one for myself. Whereas many times over the previous two or three years I'd thought about donating the couch—imagining a matter-of-fact conversation with my dad in which I told him it was time, and he absolved me of the guilt I'd feel, and we'd agree it was for the best—now that he was gone the thought was torture. I no longer had him. I would keep his couch until someone punctured a leg on an exposed spring and needed a tetanus shot, so help me God. Every time one of my children slid an arm or leg inside a rip in the fabric and tugged, making the hole bigger, I would lose my mind. "Be kind to this couch! Gentle! Your grandfather loved it!" This happened 192 times a night before bed.

I texted two upholsterers for estimates on how much it would cost to rebuild and reupholster the couch:

> It was built in 1968, and it is nine feet long. As you can see,
> the fabric needs to be replaced, and the front of the frame
> is bowing out a little. Could you give me a ballpark on what

it might cost to redo? And do you think it's worth it? I know
they don't make furniture like they used to.

I added that last part because I knew it was true, but also because
I just wanted an objective expert to tell me what to do, devoid of
filial responsibility. I wanted one of them to tell me that I was a fool
to get rid of such a sturdy, well-made frame, that the craftsmanship
was irreplaceable, that you couldn't put a price on such a piece. They
both said about $5,000, plus twenty yards of fabric.

I would have paid the money. A custom couch would cost
much more. Even something from Restoration Hardware came
close, I reasoned. Michael said to do whatever I wanted, because
he has always let me have complete control over our home's decor
and also maybe noticed that I was petting and murmuring to the
couch, like my dad's spirit was living in the armrests. Two things
stopped me from calling the upholsterers back. One, Holland
gently told me I was nuts. "You are going to spend all that money,
and you will still have a modern couch that's so low to the ground,
it's hard to stand up after sitting. It still won't be your perfect
couch," she said, which was correct, I had to admit (my mother's
English country gene was the dominant decorating trait in my
sister and me). Two, I didn't think I could feel the same way about
it once the plaid velour was gone. I'd be paying $5,000 plus the
cost of fabric for a memory.

So, if the velour was the feature I was most attached to, I would
keep that, at least. Yes, it was threadbare in spots, but the back of
the couch had been shoved against a wall for most of the couch's
life and was largely spared any wear. There was plenty of good, soft
yardage left. By the time our real estate agent told us that the kids'
bedroom would look bigger and cleaner in photos if it didn't have

an enormous rust-colored plaid couch along one wall, I was very close to being mentally ready to let go. One evening after dinner, I unzipped the cushion covers and pulled out the inserts, which had turned a peachy-beige color and had wavy brown water stains on them. Piled up on the floor, they looked like oversized makeup sponges covered in blush and foundation.

I turned the couch on its side and pulled off the paper tag that had my dad's name, Schatz, and order number on it. I refilled my drink and let myself cry for a few minutes before my kids wandered in. And then I cut a corner of the fabric with scissors and ripped it loose along one side, rough bits of orange and black thread flying into the air with the tears of an unhinged forty-four-year-old woman. We folded each section of upholstery and tucked it into a bag, then rolled up the layer of batting underneath and threw it away. I sent my mother a picture of the naked couch frame, with just a sliver of plaid along the bottom—the only piece I couldn't manage to pry off with my fingers. Good for you. Keep the fabric. Toss the couch, she texted back.

A few days later, two men on our building staff carried the couch out of the apartment in time to put it on the street for the one day of the week when the city would pick up large trash items. The next morning, as I left our house, I walked up the block, past the piles of trash bags, and saw the couch on the sidewalk. The building staff, in an attempt to make my nine-foot couch more manageable for hauling, had sawed it cleanly in half. It looked like a peanut butter sandwich folded down on itself. My heart broke.

I texted Michael a picture. Good thing I don't have second thoughts.

I have always been quick and ruthless in donating clothes or toys that don't fit in our Manhattan closets. And yet the couch haunts me. I do not know why. Lying on the couch did occasionally make me feel close to my dad, but I assume that feeling would have faded if I'd reupholstered the couch in a stain-resistant velvet. I'm fairly sure my dad would have blessed my decision, that he would not have expected me to care for and rehabilitate his furniture in his absence, as if he could live on in its broken, tattered frame. I hope he would have said to me, "Well, I'm sad to see it go, but it gave us a lot of happy years. It's time." Which, if multiplied in sorrow by a billion, was how I felt when I said goodbye to him. Still, there is a plastic trash bag in my closet bulging with scraps of rust, orange, coral, beige, and black velour awaiting its resurrection, just in case.

Like our real estate agent predicted, the bedroom did look huge once the couch was gone. Spacious. Inviting. The apartment sold in less than two weeks. And it turns out the couch was the least of my issues when it came to letting stuff go. The tears were just starting.

Chapter 2

WHAT DOESN'T KILL YOU

I COME FROM A FAMILY OF SHREWD PREPARERS. WHEN MY father died, my sister—who inherited all of his financial prudence— had a little trouble getting access to some of his accounts, as he kept changing passwords to different iterations of the names of our (long dead) dog and his first grandchild. But overall, she sifted through the will and stocks and funds with ease, because my father was fastidious. His file cabinets and manila folders were clearly labeled and dated. There were no surprises. I'm a writer, so I was little help. I was working on a minor in poetry while my sister got a business degree, and I cannot tell you what a treasury bond is. Still, I picked up a few key lessons. My father taught me to have one credit card and pay it off every month. I was in my twenties before I even knew there was such a thing as a minimum payment. You get one card, my father said, and if you can't pay it in full, you need to rethink your life choices.

Michael's parents are different. They have managed their finances just fine, not that it's any of my business, but I sense that when they die, Michael and his sisters might have to slice open some mattresses.

As a couple, we lean a bit closer to Michael's side of the family. Not that we don't pay our mortgage on time or have retirement funds. We do, although occasionally a speeding-ticket-by-mail (the ones that include a photo of the back of your minivan cruising down the West Side Highway) slips through the cracks, and we forget about it until the debt collector starts calling. But the in-case-of-death tasks—life insurance, our will—have not been a high priority.

Until we moved and packed it into a plastic IKEA bin, our last will and testament was folded into a nondescript envelope and thumbtacked to the bulletin board in our kitchen, where it had been for almost ten years. There is one copy. Michael drafted it, and only then because we were flying to California for a friend's wedding in 2011, and my mother said she would not come to New York to babysit our one-year-old, Julia, while we were gone if we didn't grow up and make a will before getting on the plane without our child.

Whenever I ask Michael if we need to update the will to include our younger children, James and Sam, or perhaps create something more official, he shrugs. "I am a lawyer. The wording includes any additional children that result from the marriage. And we had witnesses!" he says. Then I recall that he'd written the will on the flight to San Francisco, printed it at the hotel, had our friends John and Caitie sign it alongside us while sitting by the pool, and mailed it to my mother in New York. I've explained to my sister, who is the designated guardian of our children in the event of our joint deaths, that she need not locate a safe-deposit box or electronic file on a thumb drive. She just needs to find a yellowing office envelope stacked between last year's report cards and some of Sam's preschool artwork. Michael has assured me it will hold up in court.

Life insurance is a longer story. Michael's job has always offered a standard policy, and I never considered if we'd need more. Then in 2008 Michael donated a kidney to his father, and I worried that although he was the picture of health, maybe having one kidney took a sliver off his life expectancy. A few years later, after we had two children, I was on a girls' trip with my four best friends from childhood. My friend Murff mentioned that not only did her husband, Duncan, the breadwinner, have a hefty policy on himself, but he had one on her. "If I die, he's going to have to pay someone a lot of money to watch our kids," she said. I'd never thought about that. I brought up the idea to Michael that we should get more life insurance. I was a freelance writer in an industry that was slowly circling the sewer. Although I could move to Memphis with its lower cost of living and my family around to help, I preferred to stay in New York, where, unfortunately, we paid income tax. Michael said fine, he'd look into it. "It can't hurt," he said. "Even though I hardly ever get a cold. Nothing is going to happen to me."

Over the course of several years—specifically the past two—that one-kidneyed man has had four trips to the emergency room and four hospital stays, all for conditions that followed no prevailing patterns and left his doctors scratching their heads. More than once, I thought he was dead. Did I invite these traumatic health scares by demanding end-of-life paperwork? I don't like to think in superstitious terms. But as crass as it sounds, while sitting by his hospital bed on multiple occasions, I took comfort in knowing that at some point between the first and the third episodes, he finalized his supplemental life insurance policy. If ever there were two people who needed to have their affairs in order, it is a man with recurrent, bewildering medical issues and a print journalist with three children to raise.

My point is, weird things happen. And in times of uncertainty you can find your footing with faith, but it helps to have monetary backup.

"IT'S RHABDO!"

Have you ever heard of rhabdomyolysis? I didn't think so. If you are in the medical profession, please stop reading while I explain that rhabdomyolysis has something to do with your muscles feeling sore because an enzyme or maybe a protein is elevated, and if that protein runs amok unchecked, your muscles disintegrate into tattered lumps of overcooked macaroni. One weekend afternoon in 2014, Michael turned to me and said he felt extremely sore all over his body, like he'd run a marathon. He had not, by my calculations, exercised regularly in at least a year and a half, since our second child had been born and our lives had become progressively, exhaustingly hectic, so this was odd.

"Do you think it's the flu?"

"Maybe."

"Are you going to tell me you need to go to bed while I take care of our two young children and resent you for the rest of the evening?"

"Probably."

After a couple of hours, the soreness had gotten worse, and he was having trouble walking normally. We decided he should go to the closest urgent care to get checked out. His older sister,

Susan, offered to go with him. Susan is excellent in emergencies. She is levelheaded and asks good questions and can run fast, if it's required, so it was disconcerting to hear her voice on the phone a while later saying in an increasingly panicked tone, "He's in rhabdo! He's in rhabdo!"

Here is the thing about rhabdomyolysis: For the nefarious enzyme to exit your body, it has to go through your kidneys. It can damage your kidneys in the process. For a normal two-kidneyed individual, the elevated enzymes might have worked themselves out, but because Michael has only one kidney, the doctors at urgent care did not want to take any chances. According to Susan, the doctor started to freak out a tiny bit, which made her freak out even more.

"What is rhabdo? Does it have to do with rabies?" I said into the phone. Susan put Michael on. He sounded fine. The urgent care doctor wanted to send him to the ER. "Really? That seems like overkill," I said. My philosophy about diseases was that anything I'd never heard of certainly couldn't kill you, and shouldn't he just come home and rest? I called my sister's husband, Scott, who is an emergency room doctor in Charleston, South Carolina, to ask if everyone was crazy or if Michael really did need to go to the hospital. My brother-in-law is very measured and maybe the least panicky person in our entire extended family, but even he said the one-kidney thing was risky and told me, "If things get worse, he can go into kidney failure very quickly."

Susan took Michael to the emergency room at Mount Sinai, directly across the park from our apartment. For the next three days, Michael lay in a hospital bed getting fluids and watching the NFL playoffs. I guess the fluids flushed the enzyme from his system. He did not go into kidney failure. We checked out of the hospital having zero information about how rhabdomyolysis develops or why Michael was susceptible. For years we joked about it as if the entire episode was, in fact, made up—an excuse to get a break from the relentlessness of parenting small children. When one of us would feel a cold or sore throat coming on, and bedtime duties or dirty dishes hung on to us like sandbags, we'd climb into bed, pull the covers up, and say, "I can't. It's rhabdo. It's rhabdo."

"PEOPLE FAINT."

In February 2020 Michael fainted at work. We didn't think anything of it. He told me on the phone that a coworker ran in after hearing a thud and found him on the floor. Michael called his primary care physician, who suggested he come in, so I met him there. His regular doctor was not available so we saw her partner, a tight, wiry woman with close-cropped, dark, curly hair who always reminded me of Marcia Clark. This doctor took blood, ran an EKG, and checked Michael's vitals. Everything was normal. "People faint," she said. "No big deal." Go home and rest, she told him. We walked to Chick-fil-A for lunch and then took a cab back to our apartment.

Once we arrived home, Michael sat down in our living room with his computer on his lap to answer a few emails. I went into our bedroom to plug in my phone. My in-laws had come over to watch Sam, who was napping in his crib in the back of the apartment. While I was still in the bedroom, I heard my mother-in-law saying Michael's name. Not screaming, just repeating it, as if she were trying to ask him a question across a crowded room. Michael. Mike. Mike? Mike? When I went into the living room, Michael's laptop was on the floor in front of his chair, and his head had fallen back, as if he were preparing to squeeze in eye drops or have his teeth cleaned. He was staring at the ceiling, completely unresponsive.

I've seen a few dead bodies in my life—a couple of grand-parents in caskets, then my dad the moment he died in the hospital after the nurse removed the ventilator—but in all instances their eyes were closed. Michael looked like a fresh corpse. His eyes were open but glassy, and his skin was cold and damp. I shook his shoulder and held his face with both hands, screaming his name for what felt like five minutes but was probably ten seconds, until he suddenly took a huge breath, lifted his head, and looked at me. I have always thought I, like my sister-in-law Susan, would be good in an emergency. But during the minutes after Michael gasped and came back to consciousness, it became clear I am not. Twice I picked up the phone to call 911 and then hung up, deciding that was extreme. I screamed, "But you looked DEAD!" straight into Michael's face multiple times, while he was still disoriented and sweating profusely. Then I kneeled in front of his chair and asked him what he thought we should do, which at that exact moment was like asking my toddler if he had any opinions on mutual funds. I called Scott to ask what he thought. He said fainting twice in such a short period of time, especially while sitting, was odd, and we should probably go to the ER.

None of Michael's tests—brain scans, heart monitoring—showed anything strange. One of the doctors we saw mentioned the words *vasovagal syncope*, which sounded like a dance sequence or something you used to clean out a French horn. He might as well have said *bossa nova sousaphone*. I knew people who passed out at the sight of blood. My friend Hallie turned olive green and fell out of her chair in fourth grade when our teacher read to us a newspaper article about our classmate Alysia Shell's dad, a plastic surgeon, performing a groundbreaking surgical procedure. Hallie passes out giving blood, watching close-ups in a hospital drama, anything like that.

But Michael had never fainted in any type of medical situation. He didn't get dizzy when he stood up quickly or feel light-headed when he was on his feet for a long time. This couldn't be a chronic condition, I thought, and so I barely listened to the doctor describing what happens during a *Vaseline synagogue* or whatever it was. The hospital kept Michael overnight for observation, then sent him home the next day, saying his fainting might have been brought on by dehydration. That was a bite-sized explanation we could deal with. He *had* been out late at a dinner with out-of-town clients a couple of days before. They'd drunk red wine, which he rarely drinks. He did feel dehydrated. It was a fluke response, we decided. A little strange, the nurse who discharged him said, but possible.

"PEOPLE FAINT": TAKE TWO

On Father's Day, June 2021, the temperature was in the nineties, even in the morning. Michael went for a run soon after waking up, then came home, showered, and helped me get the children dressed and out of the house to attend church in person for the first time in months. It happened to be the day before we were to get a full-price offer on our apartment that we'd just put on the market—a fact that is relevant only because by brunch time, I was sure we'd never move out of that apartment together, as Michael would be deceased. We were running late to church and took a cab, squeezing all five of us into the back seat. There was some minor shifting and shoving, so it didn't register right away when Julia started grunting and pushing her father.

"Dad, get off me."

"Dad, stop. Why are you leaning on me?"

"*Ugh*. DAD."

I looked over to tell her to get a grip and noticed that Michael was keeling forward, eyes open, pale and sweaty, while Julia tried to shrug him back up to sitting by ramming her right shoulder into his chest. My immediate thought was, *Last time this happened, we missed something. And now whatever it is has killed him*. I was sure he'd had a stroke or a massive cardiac event. It did not seem farfetched that it could happen to us in our forties; in fact, I knew three women my age whose husbands had died of heart attacks in the previous couple of years.

I yelled his name. No response. The kids began pushing his arm and trying to wake him up. I banged the heel of my palm on the glass partition between me and the cabdriver and said, "You need to take us to the Mount Sinai emergency room." Just as I was screaming for the cabdriver to turn left at Eighty-Sixth Street and drive through the park to the East Side, Michael gasped. His face changed from lifeless to startled, his eyes shifting back and forth like he'd been dropped in the middle of a den of squirrels. The kids were still yelling and hitting him. The cabdriver had pulled over and was asking if he should run into the bodega on the corner for water.

"You just passed out. You were out," I said to Michael.

"No I wasn't." He looked so serious that for a second, I believed him. Good Lord, I was useless in these situations.

"Yes, yes you were. We are going to the hospital."

"What? No, don't do that," he said. At this point, sweat was beading along his hairline. He stared at me, firmly, like he was certain I was lying about what happened, like this was a prank. "Just take me home. Can we go home?"

Remembering the February before, when he fainted a second time sitting in a chair in our living room, I considered whether I wanted to watch him lose consciousness again   or have something more catastrophic happen—in front of our children. But the alternative was to check him into the ER with the three of them in tow. I told the cabdriver to make a U-turn and take us home. I called Michael's aunt Jeanne and asked her to meet us there, so that I could focus on what to do next. The cabdriver dropped us off, helping Michael out of the cab and into our lobby. We made it upstairs, and Michael lay down on our bed while I called his doctor. Again she said he was probably fine ("People faint!") but that she'd like us to go to the closest urgent care for an EKG. We took a cab from our apartment, and once we arrived, a nurse had Michael lie down on an exam table. I sat in a chair next to him while she began to attach adhesive patches connected to wires onto his neck, his chest, his shins. It was quiet; I could hear the *shhhp* of the stickers coming off the backs of each patch. And then the nurse said, "Oh, he's gone." Just like that. *He's gone.*

We were once on a flight to vacation, and as the plane began its descent, Michael excitedly turned to the kids and shouted, "Ooh, we're *goin' down*!" He immediately realized what he'd said, as a couple of passengers next to us gripped their armrests and whipped their heads toward the window. "Bad choice of words. Sorry," he said. I'd like to think the urgent care nurse thought the same thing as I lunged toward Michael's head. "Oh, he's gone." Chill tone of voice; poor choice of words.

I looked at Michael, whose head was lolling to one side of the paper-covered gurney. As I reached over and put a palm on his cheek, he came to. But not for long. Within a few minutes he passed out three more times on the exam table. All lying down, mind you. Once, he made a low gurgling sound, and his neck tensed. His foot began to point, straining forward. Two EMTs had stormed in, the sound of their heavy boots and fizzing walkie-talkies filling the small room. "He's seizing," said one. The urgent care doctor reprimanded him; apparently, it was against protocol for anyone other than her to declare certainty about a patient's condition within earshot of a loved one. "He didn't have a seizure," the doctor said, looking at me. I nodded and turned my face back to Michael. The final time he lost consciousness, he recognized the feeling and said to me, "I'm about to go." And then he did. I texted Jeanne. Sorry, we won't be home anytime soon.

Two uniformed men transferred Michael to a wheeled stretcher and directed me outside to the ambulance that was waiting to take him to the emergency room. When you ride in an ambulance with your spouse, the EMTs have to buckle you up. You can't do it yourself. That's something I know now. The seat belts in ambulances are like restraints on a roller coaster.

In the ER, nurses and doctors came and went, and Michael repeated the series of events over and over. I looked at everyone's eyes and listened to them "Hmm" and tried to gauge how hysterical I should become. Friends were texting to ask if they could bring meals. One had contacted our pastor, who was checking in, which was incredibly thoughtful. But it was also a busy Sunday. Father's Day, no less. Were we at a pastor-visiting level of seriousness? I had no idea. Couldn't a professional just tell me how much to freak out, please?

The Mount Sinai emergency room is consistently low on chairs. I gave mine up to an elderly man in the curtained bay next to us who was attending to his wife. I lifted the thin, soft tubing running from Michael's IV to the metal stand behind him and slid underneath it. He scooted a few inches so that I wouldn't roll off the edge of the inflatable hospital mattress, and we lay there—his head on the pillow, mine on his shoulder—and waited.

After a long night in the ER, his cardiologist had him admitted. The next morning we saw an electrophysiologist. (My friend Merritt, a former nurse, explained that the heart has plumbing and electricity. Cardiologists are the plumbers. Electrophysiologists are the electricians. This would prove to be the most helpful information I collected in all of our hospital stays.) The electrophysiologist told us what we had heard before. Michael appeared to suffer from vasovagal syncope, but it was strange that his fainting spells came in clusters and always when he was sitting or lying down.

Before releasing him from the hospital, his doctors decided to implant a loop recorder in his chest. "Like a grain of rice," the technician said. But it is not a grain of rice. It's bigger. Even bigger than a piece of orzo. Maybe the size of the silver, crimped part of the top of a pencil. Every time I roll over in bed and lay my face on his chest, I can feel it, a hard, knobby lump just left of center. This loop monitor, which records Michael's heart activity and alerts his doctor's office if anything out of the ordinary happens, feels completely ridiculous for what everyone thinks is just a fainting disorder. We came home with a Samsung Galaxy phone that syncs up with the monitor. A phone! That has to travel with us! And Michael has a card that he can show at the airport if a metal detector goes off, although so far one never has.

"Surely something is wrong with his heart. Why would they put in this loop recorder if something wasn't wrong with his heart? How can they not find anything?" I asked Scott on the phone, shortly before Michael was discharged.

WHAT DOESN'T KILL YOU

"It's good news that they didn't," he said. "You don't *want* them to find anything."

Ha. Oh, but I did. I did. Something small but fixable. Anything but fainting brought on by no discernible trigger that might cause him to fall onto the subway tracks. Without a definitive answer, our family entered a period of high alert. On a trip to Arkansas a couple of months after this episode, we stopped for lunch at Top's Barbecue, and when Michael didn't come out of the restroom as quickly as I anticipated, a prickly heat rose up inside me. "James! Go into the men's restroom and check on your dad. Now!" When Michael began running again, I would ask how far he was planning to go and what route he was taking. I imagined him being tended to by strangers on the road in Central Park. If Michael rested his head on the arm of the couch and didn't immediately answer the children when they asked him a question, they would rush over to him, looking for signs of life. I bought fizzy hydration tablets and would plop them into Michael's cup, saying, "Are you drinking? Drink, drink." I would save him with adequate tap water.

Every so often I would wake up in the middle of the night and watch him sleep. Michael is a loud, active sleeper. As are all of my children. They breathe as if they're blowing out dozens of birthday candles with every exhale—heavy, forceful *whooohs*. They flop like fish out of water. They wake up with wild hair. Normally, when Michael would let out a *harumph* and roll over, pulling me backward into a spooning position, I'd elbow him back to his side of the bed. Now I held his forearm across my chest and leaned back into his body, pressing every part of myself against him that I could, the backs of my knees cradling the fronts of his, my feet twisted around his toes. I listened to him breathe. The next time something went wrong, I would be listening and observing. I would catch it. We'd solve the puzzle.

Eventually, though, you get tired of keeping watch. Life goes back to normal because it has to. Eventually, I relaxed.

"BUT IS HE ALIVE?"

On Fridays I don't write. I meet a friend for coffee or take a meeting in the morning, then pick up Sam from preschool and James from fourth grade, their dismissals being an hour and a half apart. I usually drive, because Sam falls asleep immediately after preschool, and that way I can let him sleep while I park outside James's school and wait. On March 11, 2022, I was driving from one school to the next when Michael called to tell me he had fainted again at work. He'd felt it coming on and put his head down on his desk, but his desk chair was on wheels, so the minute he'd passed out, the weight of his body going limp sent the chair flying backward. He'd ended up on the floor with raw, silver dollar–sized scrapes on his forehead where he slid down the front edge of his desk.

"I think I'm okay," he said. "I'll lie down on the floor for a while and elevate my feet." Only nine months had passed since his last episode, but both of us had momentary amnesia about these faintings coming in clusters. That was a mistake.

My mother was on a plane from Memphis to New York that was meant to land in an hour. I had planned to pick up James and drive to LaGuardia Airport to get her.

"Don't try to take the subway home," I told Michael. "Why don't you stay put, and after I get my mom, I'll come by your office and pick you up on our way back."

"Sure. That sounds good. I'm going to call my doctor," he said.

I picked up James and checked the traffic to the airport. It was 2:45 on a Friday afternoon. Google Maps was predicting an hour to get there and an hour to get home. I called my mother, explained what was happening, and asked her to take a cab. "I think I should probably get Michael sooner rather than later," I told her.

Michael's office is in Midtown, just north of Times Square. There is no convenient parking in the middle of the day, so I texted him as I got closer.

> I'm on 53rd. Take your time. I'm just behind the stop sign at
> a hydrant.

He did not text me back, so after a few minutes I called. No answer. I assumed he was on the other line with his doctor, so I gave it a few more minutes and called again. Nothing.

> You okay? On phone?
> Michael, please text me.
> Text me.

I feared something was wrong, but I didn't want to panic. One, I had the boys in the car. Two, I did not want to run into the building with my hair on fire only to have Michael casually stroll off the elevator. Life is usually boring. Situations are rarely emergencies. Headaches aren't always brain tumors. My husband was almost definitely just on the phone.

I told the boys to stay in the car, and I walked into his office building, a largely empty Midtown skyscraper. The security guard at the desk smiled. I told him that my husband had a heart condition (which seemed the most efficient way to get the guard's attention) and had fainted earlier in the day. He wasn't answering my calls. I had two young children in the car outside. Could he call my husband's office and have someone on his floor check on him? My voice cracked a little as I told him the name of the law firm. I was waving my hands as I talked, and I could feel my pinkies, then my ring fingers, begin to shake, like the fringed edges of a scarf beginning to flutter in the wind. I reached forward and held on to the edge of the reception desk. The guard picked up the phone, and I listened to his one-sided conversation.

"Yes, Passarella. His wife is downstairs. She's asking if someone can reach him. Okay, he's on his way down? Okay."

"He's on his way down?" I asked. From the sound of it, whomever the security guard called had seen Michael walking out.

"Yes, he'll be down," the security guard said.

I went back to the car. I tried calling his firm's main number, but I got a recording. Most of the employees were still working remotely at least a few days a week, and hardly any came in on Fridays. Michael frequently wore running clothes to the office on Fridays so that he could jog home, and when I raised my eyebrows, he'd say, "I don't see a soul all day, trust me." The place was deserted. He was alone. No one would hear him fall to the floor.

I've called the front desk. They said you were coming down, I texted.

A few minutes passed. No Michael. No texts.

I threw on my hazards. "Boys, get out of the car and stay with me. We need to run into Daddy's office for a minute," I said.

I walked back into the building where another security guard, an older man with a thick white swoop of hair, eyed Sam suspiciously.

"Hi," I said to the nicer security guard. "Can you call up again?

I'm worried my husband has passed out. I just have a feeling. Are you sure someone checked on him?" I spoke slowly and calmly. There was a part of me that still felt it was necessary to be polite, not to cause a scene.

The security guard called the office again. "Yes, this is lobby security again. I have Mr. Passarella's wife." He put the phone on speaker. I heard the man on the other end say, "I called his office and left a message, and I sent him an email telling him his wife was downstairs." A shiver rocketed through my body, as if the temperature had suddenly dropped fifty degrees. Whoever had answered the line upstairs had misunderstood earlier. He'd never checked on Michael. He'd only gone through the normal steps of calling to let him know he had a visitor in the lobby. I leaned over the security desk and screamed into the phone. "No! I need you to physically go to his office! Please! He's on the floor of his office. Please go check on him." I looked at the security guard. "Take me upstairs. You have to let me upstairs."

There was a moment when the nice security guard looked at the older security guard for permission. Did he need to see my ID? Take my photo? Print visitor stickers?

"Are we really going to talk protocol here?" I yelled. Sam was already running toward the elevator bank, skirting under the mechanical entrance gate. "Just open these," I said, pushing against the metal arms with my hips. "You have to let me up. I have to get to him, Please," I said. *Beep.*

"What floor is he on?" asked the security guard. I had no idea. He turned and asked the other guard in the lobby, repeating the name of my husband's firm.

"Fifteen!" the other guard shouted from the desk.

I realized how little I knew about this building, his office, his coworkers. Why didn't I have anyone's number? Why didn't I know whose office was next to his? All I could remember was that there were several Steves. Heather, the wonderful human resources manager who knew everything going on in the office at all times, did not come in on Fridays. Not that it mattered. I couldn't think of anyone's last name. As we rode up in the elevator, I looked down at James, who was wide-eyed and whimpering. He knew it was bad. All I could do was squeeze his shoulder and say, "We're here now. We'll get him." My certainty that everything was probably fine because things are usually fine had vanished. Michael had always been alert enough, minutes after fainting, to call or text if he needed to. At this point it had been forty minutes since I had first texted him that I was pulling up in the car. We hadn't spoken in well over an hour. He would never ignore me, not for this long and under these circumstances.

We got off on the fifteenth floor, and the security guard stopped at the glass doors that led out of the elevator vestibule and into the office. The doors were locked. You needed a key card to enter. The guard looked at me.

"What, you don't have a card? You can't get *in*?" I screamed.

Beyond the doors I could see empty office after empty office. The lights were out. It might as well have been a weekend or holiday. As the security guard picked up the phone attached to the wall to call someone to let us in, a man came rushing down the open spiral staircase that connected the main office floor to the sixteenth, where, I learned, Michael sat. He was wearing a zip-up fleece with the firm's name embroidered on the chest. He was the office services supervisor, the guy who kept the place running, even when no one else was there. He opened the door and looked at me. His face was pale and tense. "We've called an ambulance," he said.

I stepped forward and held James behind my back.

"But is he alive? I need to know if he's alive," I said, trembling.

"Yes, he's alive."

We ran up the stairs to Michael's office, Sam yelling, "Dad? Dad? Daaad!" the entire way, oblivious to the horror of the situation and the tumbleweed of dread that was his mother barreling after him. Michael was on the floor, conscious but disoriented and bloody; he'd clearly gotten back in his chair and, once again, hit the sharp edges of his desk on the way down. His nose was bruised and swollen, and he'd bitten his tongue badly. It looked like he'd torn apart a chipmunk with his teeth. In front of him were wads of paper towels his coworker had brought him and a few scattered file folders, covered in blood. I was relieved, but I also knew this episode was different. His eyes were watery and unfocused. When I asked if he remembered what happened, he just sighed and looked at me, pleadingly. He knew who I was but not why we were there.

Michael is nine months younger than I am. When he catches up to me on his birthday every September, I relish the three months of the year when we are the same age, until my birthday in December. We're both thirty-five. We're both forty-four. I don't know why the age difference bugs me, but it does. (I'm sure it is some remnant of patriarchal norms that tell me I'm supposed to be a weaker, fairer, and younger sex.) I feel older than him in all the unwelcome, annoying ways. I'm the tougher, less playful parent. I'm the one who knows how to take apart the p-trap under the sink to find an item dropped down the drain. It's my shoulder that hurts when I sleep funny. And on top of it, I'm actually, physically older. I hit all the milestones first. First to get a colonoscopy!

But sitting on the carpet in his office, rubbing my hand up and down his leg, softly smoothing his hair back from the cuts on his forehead, saying, "You're okay. We're here. You're okay," over and over, I wished so badly he were even younger. Not just nine months. Five years younger. Ten. More. Maybe I could get old and sick and die first and never have to live a day without him.

"I hear an ambulance!" Sam said. He had climbed onto the windowsill and was happily observing the traffic below.

While we waited on the EMTs to make their way upstairs, I called Susan. She worked downtown at a high school, and I figured she might be on her way home by then. When she answered, she said she was in the East Village. I explained what happened and that I needed her to come get my car and the boys and take them home to my mother, who was by now at my apartment. I found out the next day that Susan ran several avenues over before finding an available electric Citi Bike and riding it up Sixth Avenue. She docked the bike a few blocks from Michael's office and sprinted to us just as they were loading Michael into the ambulance. Like I said: fast and good in an emergency. (And not that I would have cared, but I miraculously did not get a parking ticket, even though I had abandoned my minivan next to a fire hydrant for an hour.)

In the emergency room Michael got a call from Martha, the nurse who worked in his electrophysiologist's office. The loop recorder implanted in Michael's chest had recorded his heart activity and transmitted the information, along with some red flags or beeping or the honk of trumpeter swans—whatever the alert system was to get the staff's attention.

According to the data, Martha said, his heart had stopped for twenty-seven seconds during the last episode.

"Usually when someone has one of these episodes, I see little blips on the printout, where the heart is trying to get going again.

But not yours. It's just a flat, flat line for twenty-seven seconds," she said.

"That seems like a very long time," Michael said.

"Oh, yes. Very," said Martha.

"What made it start beating again?" Michael asked.

God, I mouthed to him.

"We don't really know," said Martha.

We spent another long night in the emergency room, although the nurses moved Michael to a quieter section where he had a television. (Still no chairs.) We watched the final games in various NCAA basketball conference tournaments. He passed out twice more, briefly, each time exhausting him further, as if the blip in consciousness required a reboot of his brain that took longer and longer each time. The nurses promised they were admitting him any minute. Hours went by. At 3:30 a.m. I discovered the marvelous news that the *New York Times* releases its new Spelling Bee word game at 3 a.m. every morning, so that gave me something to do while Michael slept. Except every time I thought about him lying on the floor of his office, alone, I sobbed and had to wipe the face of my phone dry before I could start tapping the little honeycomb of letters again. What if I'd gone to LaGuardia? How long would he have lain there in the dark?

At 4 a.m. a kind nurse named Tiffany whispered to me, "I don't know why they keep telling you they're moving him soon. It's going to be later today. Go home. I promise I'll watch him."

Sunday morning, we finally got a visit from Michael's electrophysiologist, an Indian man around our age named Dr. Varghese. I can describe our mental state at that point only as emphatically grim. We were prepared for bad news, maybe a defect in Michael's heart circuitry, maybe worse. Dr. Varghese, however, seemed chill.

He dragged over a chair from across the room and sat down. He leaned back and laced his fingers together over his chest.

Michael's condition, according to Dr. Varghese, was still vaso-vagal syncope, just a very uncommon presentation. We had two problems on our hands. Because Michael did not have a telltale trigger—seeing a needle, for example—he couldn't adjust his life-style to avoid passing out. And his response was "aggressive," said Dr. Varghese. Having the loop recorder was key. Many people with vasovagal syncope have a drop in blood pressure but nothing more. We knew from the loop recorder data that Michael's heart stopped for significant periods, which was supposedly not fatal but still sounded apocalyptic every time we said it out loud.

"You aren't worried that my heart stopped for that long?" Michael asked.

"Well, everyone else on your case is very concerned about the long heart pauses," Dr. Varghese said. "But no, I'm not."

"I think that's bananas," I said.

Dr. Varghese shrugged. "In all my years of treating patients with vasovagal syncope, I don't know anyone who has died from it. It's the repercussions that are dangerous. You know, hitting your head or having a car accident." So Michael likely was not going to die from a heart problem; we would just live in terrorized fear of secondary death from fainting for the rest of our days.

"We can't do *nothing*, though, right?" Michael asked.

"Well, we could do nothing, but I don't think that's the best idea for you," said Dr. Varghese.

One treatment option was to put in a pacemaker, which would restart his heart if necessary but could not prevent the fainting, which really seemed like the whole point, in my interpretation. The other was a new procedure, an ablation, that zapped nerves around the heart so that they would stop communicating with the nervous system. A doctor in Brazil had been doing it for years and it was gaining popularity in Europe, but very few hospitals in the United States used it as a treatment. Fortunately, Dr. Varghese and the electrophysiology team at Mount Sinai did. And he thought Michael was a good candidate. We could always put in a pacemaker down the road if necessary.

"Take a few days to think about it," said Dr. Varghese. We did, calling around for second opinions. Merritt's cousin, an electrophysiologist in Nashville, said his group had heard of the ablation and thought the results were promising, but no one at Vanderbilt was trained to do it yet. Scott did some research and gave us a thumbs-up. A third doctor, an electrophysiologist in New Jersey who was a friend of one of Michael's coworkers, said it was too experimental, and he recommended doing nothing. I pondered that for a moment and wondered if I'd ever again relax watching Michael play in the ocean with Sam, if I'd ever again be okay with him driving our kids. My driving the car is such a rare occurrence—because I hate driving and am not great at it—that every time I sit behind the wheel, Sam asks, "Wait, Mom. Are you sure you know how to work this thing?" We decided on the ablation.

A few days later, on St. Patrick's Day, I sat in the waiting room on the fifth floor of the hospital watching TV with four other families, all of us waiting for a nurse to come through the door and call out our loved one's name. I watched the first half of a March Madness matchup between my alma mater, the University of North Carolina, and Marquette. I bought snacks from the vending machine. I was so out of sorts that I forgot to watch the second half of the game. I just didn't pull it back up on my phone. The next day Michael mentioned the final score. "Oh, they won?" I said.

A nurse came through the doors around 7:45 p.m. I had kissed Michael goodbye at the reception desk almost five hours before. He texted me when the anesthesiologist arrived, so by my calculations, he'd been under for a little more than three hours. "Elizabeth?" the nurse said. "Yes! Me! Coming!" I grabbed my coat, backpack, snacks, and book in an unruly heap in front of my chest and began to shuffle toward the door with my knees clamped together to hold the Reese's Peanut Butter Cups that were falling out of my lap, when I realized that another family was also gathering their belongings (in normal fashion) and looking at me. Then I remembered. The nurses were calling out the names of the patients, not the family members. Patient Elizabeth, this family's loved one, was out of surgery. Patient Michael, mine, was not. I sat down. Around 8:15 p.m., Dr. Varghese called me. Everything had gone exactly as they'd hoped.

"Michael?" the nurse at the door said, finally.

The next morning, before the hospital discharged him, Michael talked to another doctor, a fast-talking woman who worked in Dr. Varghese's office. "It went great! If you were anywhere else, you'd have a pacemaker, but how lucky are we that we are at one of only two or three hospitals in the whole country that does this procedure?" she said, waving her hands enthusiastically. "It's just a perfect solution! It's so elegant! Of course, we have no long-term studies, so how will it hold up in ten years? Ha! Who knows, right?" She held her palms up, smiled widely, and walked out. Did we ask her about the long-term effectiveness of the procedure? I can't remember. All I know is that ten years felt like a lifetime away, and all I wanted was the flood of fear to be dammed up in the immediate present. I wanted them to find something, and they didn't. I wanted them to do something, and they did. I would not be greedy with assurances.

I have a strange lump just under the skin of my abdomen, a couple of inches below my belly button. It has been there for a long time, around nine years. I first noticed it when I was pregnant with James, and the skin of my abdomen was stretched as tight as a piece of Saran Wrap over a bowl of potato salad. Then it was the size of a pea. Now it's like a pecan half. It does not hurt, but it is noticeable when I'm wearing a bikini. My dermatologist and gynecologist have both poked at it and declared that it's almost certainly a benign fatty deposit. But last Christmas my sister planted a little seed of doubt. "What if it's a tumor full of hair?" she asked.

This is a running joke between the two of us. A few years ago she read a news story about a woman who had an ovary removed, and when the doctors cut open the ovary, they found a giant hair ball. I have a thing about hair that is not attached to a body, in the sense that it skeeves me out. I don't like baths because hairs float on top, just waiting to slide onto you. On a ski trip one year when we were kids, my mother turned on the condominium's Jacuzzi, and a bunch of medium-sized hair balls shot out of the jets. I've never recovered. I've woken up in a panic from nightmares where a hair is wrapped around one of my molars, and I can't get it loose. My sister finds this aversion ripe for exploiting. She likes to remind me that there are cells in our body that are neutral, that can morph into something specific over time, like nerve cells or fingernail cells. Hair cells. That's how the woman ended up with an ovary full of hair. Those clean-slate cells decided to organize. So, she said to me, how do you know that lump isn't, like, a set of baby teeth?

Sometime in 2021, in between Michael's first and second rounds of fainting, I had my own appointment at Mount Sinai. I went to see a general surgeon about the mysterious lump. My primary care physician first suggested I have an ultrasound, but the results of the ultrasound were inconclusive. "It looks like they don't know what the heck it is," she said. "Go see a surgeon."

That's how I ended up in Dr. Park's office. While I waited for him, I chatted with his assistant.

"Did you look at the ultrasound?" I asked her.

"Oh, I think Dr. Park is looking at it now," she said.

"Do you think there's a chance it's not just cartilage? Maybe it's something weird? Like teeth?"

"I'm sorry?"

"Teeth. The bridge of a nose. I don't know."

The assistant stared at me, wondering, I assume, if I was serious. She laughed gently.

"No, I don't think so."

I believed her, and I didn't ask Dr. Park. I trusted him when he told me it was, in fact, fatty tissue, no matter what the ultrasound did or did not show, and that it was harmless. He could cut it out in a few minutes with some numbing medication, he said. I told Dr. Park I would think about it, that it didn't bother me, so maybe scheduling a surgery—even a tiny one—for vanity's sake wasn't necessary. I walked home through Central Park with one hand tucked into my waistband, resting on that weird little lump.

Medicine is murky. Doctors are human. Research changes. No one can tell me the socially acceptable level of panic in a given health crisis. I've asked. Every morning I button my pants over the nodule in my abdomen and think: *There's a millionth of a percent chance that I'm carrying around a sac with an itty-bitty thumb inside.* There's a slight chance my husband faints and falls in front of a bus. Most likely he won't. But I can't be absolutely certain.

John Green wrote in his book *The Anthropocene Reviewed* about having viral meningitis. "The virus that spread through my spinal fluid had no meaning; it did not replicate to teach me a lesson, and any insights I gleaned from the unsharable pain could've been learned less painfully elsewhere." I haven't asked Michael if his vasovagal syncope episodes have taught him anything or changed his perspective on life in any significant manner that he couldn't have gleaned from another experience. It may be too soon. So far he's still reminding himself that if he feels funny, he should immediately drop to the floor. Head-on-desk has proved a dangerous position.

But I've learned a few things by virtue of proximity and the fact that, between the two of us, I've remained conscious for it all. I've learned how to go on living our life by faith, which should not be a hard concept for a person of deep faith, which I am. I believe in all kinds of things I cannot see—God, the Holy Spirit, angels, the devil, and that I know for certain where I go when I die. And yet it is so often quite hard to step out before first locking down the known facts. I've been reminded, during some of those dark, unsleepable nights in emergency rooms, that I will rest on faith as a last resort if at all possible. First (and second and third), I will try to control everything. I will badger medical professionals for rational answers.

Sometimes there are none. We don't get certainty, even in science. No one can tell me why Michael's heart started beating again after twenty-seven seconds. I wanted an illustrated diagram. I got a mystery. Would it be wise for me to learn CPR? Probably, yes. Might I attempt it when my husband is just a bit too still for a bit too long while lying on the couch? Also yes. But there's no harm in being prepared. I have resisted the urge to put babyproofing bumpers on the corners of his office desk. I now have the cell phone numbers of four of Michael's coworkers who sit nearest to him. Only one is named Steve.

I've loved my husband since about four days after we met. Watching him play dead and come back to me over and over these past two years has shown me moments, mere seconds, of what it would be like if I lost him suddenly. And I appreciate every day that he wakes up and rolls toward me. I have faith in new things unseen: a collection of crispy, burnt nerve endings that, I hope, will keep his heart safe. The words of a doctor who tells us it's not fatal.

Every morning now Michael leaves the apartment to take James to school, and I say, "Goodbye, be careful, don't stand anywhere near the edge of the subway platform, I love you." And he says, "I will text you when I drop him and when I get to work." And he does. And I will never again take it for granted.

Chapter 3

FINDING LOIS

Moving: Part 1

MOST PRUDENT PEOPLE SELL THEIR HOMES WHEN THEY HAVE an idea of where they'll be moving and a plan for how to get there. We sold our apartment because the New York real estate market seemed to be on a hot streak, and I had one promising conversation with an elderly woman who said her late husband told her—from heaven—that our family was supposed to buy her place.

It didn't start with her deceased husband, though. It started with a letter I wrote. I couldn't have known the long and complicated road we would navigate when it came to this new apartment, but I did get the ball rolling.

Actually, now that I really think about it, it started with our roof deck.

Our building is right next to Central Park and is about twenty floors high. The buildings on either side are shorter, so if you live on a high floor of our building, you have clear views of the treetops and, depending on the angle, the Empire State Building. From the roof of our building, you can see all the way to Queens and from the top of Central Park at 110th Street to the bottom at Columbus Circle. Our roof wasn't open to residents, however, because the flooring wasn't reinforced, and while there was a wrought iron fence around the edge, our building's insurance didn't cover people socializing twenty floors in the air without adequate safety enhancements. I'm told that years ago, before we moved in, people would climb the stairs anyway and hang out in secret.

In my first New York apartment building, which was only six stories high, we did that all the time. The steel door that led to the roof bore a sign alerting us to an alarm, but that alarm was never armed. We pushed the door open, hung string lights, and threw parties up there. It was the second place I kissed my husband when we started dating. On New Year's Eve 2000, my friend Thomas took his clothes off and screamed, "I'm the king of the world!" from the edge overlooking Second Avenue. Roofs in New York City, if you can get to yours, are like an extra room or a backyard. If your building is nice enough to have a finished roof deck with pavers and landscaping and Adirondack chairs, you are probably at an age where your friends don't get naked at your parties anymore.

During the pandemic our building decided to turn the unfinished roof into a proper, usable deck. I was unusually privy to the details because Michael was on our co-op board, which was normally not at all exciting for me, because he took it seriously and wouldn't spill any gossip. But in this case I managed to get a few private trips to the roof during landscaping and gave an opinion on the furniture. When the new roof deck finally opened in

April 2021, its presence coincided with the beginnings of a vaccine rollout, warmer weather, and a reprieve from some of the Covid restrictions we'd been living with in the city.

Neighbors who hadn't socialized in a year brought up their dinners on trays, opened bottles of wine, and acted genuinely thrilled to see each other. The view was so expansive that you could watch the sunset over the Hudson River, and everyone from families with small children to elderly residents who had hardly left the building in months came up, eager for fresh air and a chance to drink cocktails in the presence of actual human beings. Once it got dark, small lanterns tucked in the planting boxes came on just as the lights in Midtown began to twinkle. There were pergolas with climbing vines. There was Wi-Fi!

Some nights every table was full, and it looked like the most glowy, glamorous restaurant in New York. Michael and I stopped caring about going out, just the two of us; we could simply put the kids to bed and take a drink to our roof. My mother visited shortly after it opened, and she said what I'd been thinking for weeks: "Well. You can't move *now*."

We didn't have to move, to be clear. Our apartment had two bedrooms, and we had three children, but as I tell anyone who raises an eyebrow about having kids in city apartments, families across the globe live in smaller spaces with more people and consider themselves extremely fortunate. We were doing fine. But being home all together during the pandemic had stretched the limits of our optimism when it came to square footage. Our youngest child was sleeping in a walk-in closet (which he liked, I promise), but we knew that when he outgrew his crib, we'd need to find alternate arrangements. More importantly, two old friends of ours, both real estate agents, said it was prime time to sell. Apparently New York was not dead; it was molting. Everyone emerged from lockdown, peeled off their own four walls like shapewear at the end of a wedding, and went looking for something roomier.

My dream had always been to stay in our building but find a bigger apartment. After the roof deck was finished, the desire intensified. I had lived in our apartment longer than I had lived in any home, even the one where I spent the bulk of my childhood. I'd cried in front of the doormen countless times. I'd discovered one of my favorite novels on the lending library shelf in the laundry room. Once, when a water main broke on our street and I couldn't get to my car because of the flood, our building manager, Jeff, grabbed my keys from my hand, ran through a rushing river of brown water, backed my car up the one-way street, and pulled it around the block so that I could get to soccer pickup on time. I was attached.

Unfortunately every three-bedroom apartment in the building faced the park, which is like saying a perfectly lovely black dress is also trimmed in gold-dipped hummingbird wings. Even when one would come up for sale, it would be way out of our price range. Then one morning in March, as we were talking to Jeff in the lobby, he mentioned an apartment on the first floor. He gestured to the door, which was just past the package room with two steps leading up to it. We'd never seen anyone come or go from there. I'd heard it had been converted to an office—many residential buildings have medical offices on the first floor—and was on the small side, a two-bedroom like the other apartments in that line.

"Oh, no, it's big," said Jeff.

"How big?" Michael asked.

"I mean, it's in pretty bad shape, you know. No one's lived in it for ages."

"How big?" I asked.

"I have to go in to look at one of the pipes. Want to just come in with me?"

The apartment belonged to Lois. Lois's husband owned it before they got married, and the two of them never lived in it together. Her husband used the apartment as a medical office. Apparently, a few of our doormen used to go to him as their primary care doctor. According to Jeff, Lois lived elsewhere in the city but paid the maintenance on this apartment on time every month.

"She's a very nice woman. Shows up occasionally to check on things," said Jeff, pushing open the back door that led from the garbage and recycling area into the apartment's kitchen. He held a flashlight over his head as the three of us walked in.

The kitchen—the entire apartment, really—smelled like a chest of old quilts and knitted afghans that you've opened up after many years to find that the cat most definitely peed in it a while back. I have spent a lot of time in nursing homes with grandparents, great aunts, and, for a season, the residents of the Dewitt Nursing Home on East Seventy-Ninth Street, where I helped lead a worship service on Sundays. If you took the odors of stale flesh, gravy, and dirty sheets but removed the antiseptic smell of hand soap that permeates the halls, you'd have some combination that felt familiar to what we experienced in Lois's apartment. It could have been worse.

But then. There was the stuff. In the kitchen, which was covered in linoleum and yellowing subway tile, drawers were crammed with papers, tools, and old rags. Two refrigerators were humming, fully functioning. (It would be months before I had the courage to open one of them and see what was preserved inside—oddly, a lot of Nips coffee candy and Cheez-Its.) In the next room two dining tables were sandwiched together on their sides, with dozens of chairs piled next to them. There were several heavy wooden desks and all kinds of medical equipment: metal cabinets full of drugs, privacy curtains that looked like props from a World War II–era hospital drama, wheelchairs, oversized exam lamps. The bathrooms were covered in plaster and broken tiles. Stacks of magazines five feet high lined the foyer and a home office. One closet was almost entirely filled with phones—new ones still in the box and old rotary ones in different colors. Black, cream, olive green. There were unopened leaf blowers and ceiling fans, tools, and boxes full of thousands of syringes. In one room we had to suck in and shimmy between the wall and a tower of cardboard boxes that was leaning ominously toward us at the tippy-top. The last part of the tour was a skinny hallway off the master bedroom (huge, by the way), which led to a narrow bathroom that housed, in addition to many, many more boxes, a glass gallon jar of apple cider and two garden hoses.

Michael and I wanted it. All of it. Immediately. The apartment was easily two thousand square feet, as big as any of the three-bedrooms on higher floors. But this one was falling apart. It wasn't just the hoarder-level clutter; the walls were crumbling. Maybe in this condition we could afford it. We kept looking at each other with saucer eyes. How had we never known this apartment existed, right under our noses? Why had we never investigated? Who would let this place sit here without trying to sell it?

Michael got Lois's number from the building management company and called her the next day. He explained who he was, that we lived in the building and had three children, that we desperately wanted to stay in the building, that her apartment was probably our only opportunity. If she ever considered selling it, would she please let us know? She told Michael that she thought it was time to sell, actually, but she had felt overwhelmed after her husband's death and couldn't deal with the task of emptying out the place and getting it on the market. The only problem, she said, was that another man in the building had called her a few years before, asking to buy it. She felt she needed to give him first right of refusal. Michael said that was fine, gave her his number, and hung up. Then we did what many New Yorkers who become obsessed with getting a deal on an undervalued apartment would do: ticked through the different neighbors we knew who might be standing in our way and plotted to quietly poison them. And then I wrote Lois a letter.

If you are a writer by profession and have heard a single story, real or fictional, about someone scoring their dream house in the middle of a bidding war because they wrote the sellers a heartfelt letter, well, you have no choice. *We would love to continue raising our children in this building*, I wrote to her. *We love the city, the neighborhood, the park, and the staff who work here. It would be such a gift for us to restore your apartment and make it a home.* I'm not going to deny that it was cheesy and slightly manipulative. But it was also all true. And legal. I wrote down my email address and cell phone number as well as Michael's so that she could get in touch with us, mailed the letter, and tried to temper my expectations. Lois had sat on this place for almost eight years. Someone else might already have a claim on it. Why did I think she would suddenly have a change of heart?

One afternoon, about a week later, my phone rang.

"Hello, Elizabeth?" Her voice was clear and strong. It lilted up at the end of every phrase.

"Yes! This is Elizabeth."

"Aw, hello." (She drew out her vowels, so that words lingered, like a car that was slowly rolling to a stop.) "This is Lois. I got your letter."

"Oh, I'm so glad. Thank you for calling," I said.

"Yes. Well, I wanted to talk to you. I talked to your husband last time. He called me, you know. But I like talking to women better than men," she said.

"Of course. That sounds good to me. I'm happy to talk to you." *If I can just be the most pleasant and polite and comforting person I've ever managed to be*, I thought, *she will love me, and she will see we are good people*. I held my breath and hoped she could feel me smiling, anticipating, on the other end.

"Sure, sure. Okay, so I got your letter. I just loved it. It was such a beautiful letter. And I'm not even going to call that other man who asked me if he could buy the place. I'm going to sell the apartment to you. My husband, he was a good man, he died. And listen, he looked down on me from heaven and told me that your family is supposed to bring that apartment back to life. Okay?"

"Okay," I said.

Chapter 4

BUT, YOU KNOW, POLISHED

ALL I WANTED WHEN I MOVED TO NEW YORK IN 1999 WAS TO be a food writer. Specifically, I wanted to be Ruth Reichl. Reichl was the restaurant critic for the *New York Times*, but it wasn't even her restaurant reviews that interested me the most. In 1998 she published her first memoir, *Tender at the Bone*, and that book changed my life. A few years later I discovered Calvin Trillin, who could write an entire essay about a very specific type of bagel that he could no longer find in his Greenwich Village neighborhood, only the essay was really about trying to get his daughter to move back to New York from the West Coast. She'd come home, she said, if he could find the pumpernickel bagel she loved as a child that no one seemed to be making anymore. The piece was about family and how painful new life stages can be. *Tender at the Bone* wasn't really about food, either. The kitchen was a gateway to stories of longing and belonging and class and love. I was a Southerner descended from New York Jews on my father's side. I knew food, and I knew how to tell a funny story. Ruth Reichl showed me that you could use one to get to the other, and that was all I wanted to do.

The summer I read *Tender at the Bone*, I took an internship at *Southern Living* magazine in Birmingham. My co-intern, Paige, and I were assigned to the food department, where we answered phones all day.

"Hello, *Southern Living* food department, this is Elizabeth. How can I help you?" I said over and over, day in, day out.

"Oh, honey. Hi. This is Marjorie Putnam. I'm callin' from Jackson. Now, I think I've lost my mind, but I cannot for the life of me find a recipe for a chicken pot pie that I saved from one of your issues."

"I'd be happy to help. Do you remember what issue it was from?"

"Well, that's a good question. It was from a while ago. I had that magazine in a stack on my kitchen counter, and I think I must have thrown it away by accident. I want to say it was orange. It might have had some mums on the cover."

"Okay, so that sounds like maybe a fall issue. Probably October."

"You know, I think you're right. But a few years ago. I've made this chicken pot pie a dozen times. You'd think I'd memorized the recipe by now, but I haven't!"

Then I would take down the caller's number and address and start looking for the recipe. No magazines in 1998 had websites or electronic databases. All of the recipes that had run in *Southern Living* were listed on index cards and stored in a card catalog, just like a library, that ran along one wall of the food department. Paige or I would take whatever information the caller could give us—the recipe ran the summer of her daughter's wedding, so . . . 1993; the cover definitely had a cake on it; she remembered a story about an alligator wrangler—to narrow our search. Nevermind that Mrs. Putnam could have been recalling a recipe that ran in *Good Housekeeping* for all I knew.

I'd start five or six Octobers back, thumbing through the cards in the long wooden drawers, looking for pot pie. When I found the recipe, I'd locate the corresponding issue in a different storage room, photocopy the recipe, attach a handwritten note on *Southern Living* stationery, and mail it out. Other than eating lunch in the test kitchen every day and sampling Thanksgiving and Christmas menus (that's what food magazines are working on in the heat of the summer), Paige and I spent the majority of our time that summer looking for a lemon bar that was definitely pictured next to a glass of iced tea with a pool in the background, or a dip that might have had dehydrated onions in it, or maybe not but you were supposed to serve it with Fritos.

Some recipes were frequent fliers. We got two or three calls a week about Hummingbird Cake, *Southern Living*'s most requested recipe, so we had a file folder filled with photocopies ready to go. And we were well-versed on the troublemakers; one cake that called for 7-Up would fall flat if the cook used Sprite. When we received an angry phone call about it, we would ask if by chance the caller had substituted Sprite or Sierra Mist, and we were so very sorry, but the recipe would not work as promised. Very infrequently we got a frantic caller who was in the middle of making something that was not rising or browning as promised. She (always she) was standing in front of the oven, and things did not look right. Could we help? Paige and I knew our limits. We would politely ask if we could put the person on hold and then sprint across the floor to find Donna or Denise, our mentors and seasoned food editors, or, if we were in extremely dire straits, a member of the test kitchen staff, and one of them would take the call.

The next fall I joined the staff at the *Daily Tar Heel*, my college newspaper. Other writers had been working at the *DTH* for two or three years, putting in time covering budgets or campus construction so that they could finally, as upperclassmen, cover the arts or be investigative reporters. I took a chance showing up as a senior having never before darkened the door. And I had no interest in news—I was already writing editorials and city council roundups in my journalism classes. What I wanted, I told the editor, was to write restaurant reviews. The *DTH* had never had a food critic, and if I was going to be a food writer in New York after graduation, I needed some clips. My pitch was that Chapel Hill was known to be a good food town, and students would be well served to know what restaurants to book for dates or parents' weekend. I said I would pay for my own meals; the paper did not have to give me a budget, just a column. The editor said yes.

For the rest of the school year, I reviewed everything from a newly opened Roly Poly sandwich shop to Crook's Corner, a James Beard Award winner. I tried to be mostly positive and balanced, but I was also naive. One Cuban restaurant, after receiving a less-than-favorable review, blasted me for being ignorant about their cuisine (fair—although the service was also terrible). For the rest of the year, whenever my friends wanted to meet there for drinks (the drinks were a bright spot), the owner refused to let me in. If I somehow slipped through to the outdoor patio, he'd come back yelling and wagging a finger at me until I left.

In the early spring I wrote to Ruth Reichl to tell her how meaningful her book had been to me and ask if the *New York Times* food section was hiring. She wrote me back a lovely, warm note to say no, but that I should stop by the *Times* office and say hello when I got to the city. I never had the chance. A month later she announced she was leaving to be the editor in chief of *Gourmet*. I tried to work there, too, but the closest I got was another magazine owned by Condé Nast: *Vogue*. (To get this out of the way: I enjoyed working at *Vogue*. Anna Wintour was intimidating but perfectly nice to me. My writing improved. I met some fascinating people.)

My job at *Vogue* was as an associate beauty editor. I was qualified for that job because I'd spent a couple of years as an assistant beauty editor at *InStyle*. I was qualified for *that* job because I was willing to do anything and available to start immediately. Before *InStyle* I lived on Long Island and worked as an intern at *Newsday*, the regional paper. As that internship neared its predetermined end, I sent resumes to every magazine human resources department in Manhattan. There happened to be an opening in the beauty department at *InStyle*. When I interviewed, neither the beauty editor, Eleni, nor her boss, the beauty director, Kim, seemed to be wearing makeup. Neither asked me if I cared about skin care or hair care or spas. Eleni was a folklore and mythology major at Harvard. Magazines in the early aughts were full of people like that, people who were curious and talented enough to write about *anything*—retinol (still the gold standard twenty-five years later, by the way), wedge sandals, or celebrities—and make it read like a fast-paced novel or a hilarious editorial. The subject didn't matter. The words did. Rumaan Alam, the award-winning author of *Leave the World Behind*, once wrote this in *New York* magazine about his time at *Lucky*:

> That I worked as a writer at *Lucky* never impressed a single person in the business, which is a shame because *Lucky*'s voice and

style (brevity, an insistent avoidance of repetition) taught me a hell of a lot about writing, possibly more than my undergraduate writing workshops. If you think I am overstating it, try writing 24 captions about essentially identical black shoes, or beaded handbags, or two-piece bathing suits; you can't repeat a word among those, and the construction of each must be different, otherwise the editor-in-chief is going to throw a red pen at you. It's like playing word Jenga, or composing tidy, little fashion haikus.

I never lied in my *InStyle* interview. I never said I was a makeup and skin care aficionado. I told the truth: that I was a hard worker, a fast learner, and I couldn't believe there was a magazine that would let me see the inside of celebrities' homes. This was before social media and, really, the internet in general, as it exists today; if you wanted to know what a celebrity was doing or wearing, you read *People* or *Us Weekly* or *InStyle*. I loved the behind-the-scenes details about famous lives, and at *InStyle* we had the phone numbers of every makeup artist on every television and movie set. It felt like half of my time in the office involved calling the hairstylist for *Friends* to discuss Jennifer Aniston's current look. For years Nicole Kidman's former hair guru cut mine. For free. Even a woman as apathetic about beauty as I was couldn't resist the spa services and face creams and expensive shampoos, especially when I could not have afforded any of it on my salary. Those were the perks of working in the beauty department. Good hair and a Shu Uemura eyelash curler.

When I saw that *Vogue* had an opening, I applied, with the reasoning that although the job was still in the beauty department, it was a step up, title-wise. And *Vogue* felt, to me, as serious as you could get in the women's magazine world. The magazine ran heavy political profiles and travel stories. Maybe I could move sideways from beauty to one of those departments. Julia Reed wrote for *Vogue*, and she came up from the Mississippi Delta and talked with an accent thicker than my mother's. Part of me always worried that being Southern was somehow a detriment in the New York media world. A stupid notion, considering that right around that time the executive editor of the *New York Times* was from Alabama and my friend Sid Evans of *Southern Living*, who is from Memphis, was the editor in chief of *Field & Stream*. But if Julia Reed was welcome at *Vogue*, surely I could make it. As a copy test, the beauty director asked me to write a short piece about the season's new lip color. If I remember correctly, I spent a large chunk of my word count comparing it to unrelated items, like a child's juice box. She called me for an interview. We got along well. And then she explained that I had to meet Anna.

In 2017 *New York* magazine published an article titled "What 10 People Wore to Their Interviews with Anna Wintour," a follow-up to the equally popular 2012 story, "What 13 People Wore to Their Interview with Anna Wintour." What is striking to me reading them now is not the outfits; most interviewees went through the same thought process and landed on tactics similar to mine in 2001. It's that few of the people were bigwigs. These were men and women interviewing to be assistants and junior staff writers. Anna did not just take time out of her schedule to interview art directors or senior fashion editors. She interviewed everyone. Maybe some see that as controlling. I thought it was generous.

Two things ended up being my saving grace for my meeting with Anna. One, I was ignorant about fashion and, to some extent, how powerful *Vogue* really was in the industry. Like a dumb baby lamb who wanders into a wolf's den not knowing that she could be dinner, I flat-out didn't know enough about Anna Wintour to be nervous meeting her. Two, my friend Amy Powell, the assistant fashion editor at *InStyle*, gave me a list of rules. If I couldn't afford to wear a designer that was currently beloved by the editors of *Vogue* (I could not, not by a long shot), then I should wear something well-tailored and forgettable, but not a suit. My shoes should look like Manolo Blahniks or Jimmy Choos, even if they were Steve Madden. My bag, if it couldn't be an "it" bag of the moment (it could not, not by a long shot), should be black and nondescript, so as not to draw attention. Now was not the time to get funky and carry a tote made from one of your great aunt's afghans. And when Anna asked me why I wanted to work at *Vogue*, I should never, ever say that *Vogue* covered fashion or politics or trends in a way I admired. I should say *Vogue* sets the fashion and politics and trends. *Vogue* says what's important. Then everyone else covers it. "Repeat that to me," Amy said, getting at my eye level so I knew she was serious.

Amy did not tell me to spend an hour in the "career woman" section of Lord & Taylor looking at patterned, polyester blouses. But I always found Lord & Taylor to be a reliable bet, the break-fast buffet of department stores in Midtown Manhattan. Saks was too expensive; its inventory bottomed out with brands like Theory, which was still too high-end for me. Bloomingdale's had a nice, well-priced selection, but the store was always chaotic, whereas Lord & Taylor felt like you'd arrived just after everyone exited for a fire drill. If you wanted designer, you could find it, but most of the real estate was filled with smart separates and nondescript knitwear. I did not want to take a risk with something trendy and bomb. *Tailored, not too businesslike, forgettable.* I tried on a stack of shirts and chose a diaphanous button-down with red and royal blue teardrops on a black background. It would work with my black straight-leg pants. I found some pointed-toe, skinny-heeled black pumps that cost around $120, but before I put down my credit card I called my boyfriend (now husband) crying that I couldn't believe I was buying an expensive pair of shoes I could barely afford just to impress an editor for five minutes. "Who cares? Do what you have to do to get the job," he said. "They're black heels, not clown shoes. You'll wear them again." I tucked my writing portfolio—nothing was digital back then; writers carried around leather-bound binders full of photocopied clips that they often messengered over to editors in advance of the interview—in a boxy black Coach bag that my mother gave me for my college graduation.

The best part of the blouse I bought was that the sleeves were loose and flowing, so sweat could roll down the sides of my torso into my waistband rather than pool in the fabric under my arm-pits. While I waited in the reception area at *Vogue*'s offices in the 4 Times Square building, it was deathly quiet. All I heard was the click-clack of high heels on the hard floors.

Before I went in to see Anna, I met Laurie Jones, the managing editor, who had a no-nonsense, Hillary Clinton vibe. She wore a red pantsuit and asked me what was the last book that I'd read. "*The Liars' Club* by Mary Karr," I said, which was half true. I'd read the first twenty or so pages. Laurie paused, never looking up from my resume, while I held my breath, willing her to move on to something else and not ask me a single thing about the plot of *The Liars' Club*. "That's a good answer," she said. "Mary Karr is from Texas. I'm from Texas." Whew. There was a feeling I'd come to know well during my short time at *Vogue*, of giving just enough of a right answer to win a second of approval, and you could slip out the door on that approval if you had the sense to keep your mouth shut. Under normal circumstances, when a person brought up being from Texas, I'd launch into a conversation about my aunts and uncles who lived in Houston and Dallas before bringing up the regional preferences of beef versus pork barbecue. I was like a wind-up toy in these situations. *Let me loose, and I'll tap-dance through a delightful conversation about our shared experience!* But something told me to shut up and sit still. Finally Laurie looked up, slapped her hands on the desk, and stood up to walk me back to her assistant's cubicle.

"Okay, then. I'll have Sophie here walk you down to Anna."

The meeting was short, and I don't remember much. As God is my witness, I did say one thing that made Anna chuckle, and if I could recall what it was, I'd have it engraved on a plaque. (What I did take away was the impression that she was a normal human who appreciated a funny line. Lore has it that you were never supposed to speak to Anna in an elevator. I did half a dozen times. "Good morning, Anna," I'd say if I happened to get on with her from the lobby. "Good morning, Elizabeth," she'd reply every time. Normal human stuff.) My chair was stiff and spindly. I tried to tuck my Coach bag underneath it, and it wouldn't fit. Anna wore a short-sleeved crewneck sweater with a pencil skirt. At the end, she asked some version of why I wanted the job, and I was ready. I told her that I wanted to work at *Vogue* because I thought it was full of excellent writing. And because *Vogue* didn't report on the trends. It set them.

She stood up and extended her hand. "Well, Amy [the beauty director] likes you," she said. I got the job.

The editors of *Vogue*, including my excellent boss, Amy Astley, and Anna, *did* know good writing. That part was true. *Vogue* is the only magazine I've written for that did not assess your story according to how it would fit in bulleted pieces alongside check-lists and sidebars or flow around a set number of explanatory photographs. With feature stories, you wrote the piece, the art department found an archived Irving Penn photograph that could be vaguely tied to the subject matter, and the words spilled around it, like pouring ganache over a cake. If there were too many words, they continued in the back of the issue: "*LIPS, con't from page 122.*"

Magazine readers and advertisers both prefer long captions and tons of product pictures, it turns out, but at that time *Vogue* was powerful and rich enough not to give a rip. I wrote thousands of words about eyebrow threading, which of course has been around for centuries but had yet to break through to the world of white beauty editors. My editor sent me to Chinatown to try what she'd been told was a "string facial." I sat on a cushion in the living room of an elderly Chinese woman, who zipped and pulled the twisted string across every millimeter of my face, from my forehead down to my clavicle. I'd entered her apartment with no idea what the treatment entailed, so having a woman moving her face in a peck-ing motion so close to mine that our eyebrows rubbed together was paralyzing. I didn't know where she'd stop. My belly button? Several times she paused to say, "Tough. Tough," after breaking a string on my wiry sideburns. I'd heard the same thing from a bikini waxer. "You look fair, but you have some Eastern European in you, no?" she'd declared. The first draft of that threading story was terrible. I began with a deep dive into my hair removal history, includ-ing weekly electrolysis in college and one at-home waxing disaster where I chickened out on pulling off the strip and attempted to slowly dissolve the wax with hot water and rubbing alcohol. Many editors would just rewrite your piece. Amy was patient and encour-aging. She gave nudges and suggestions and extra time until I landed on a draft good enough to send to Anna. It came back with the blessed seal of approval: "AWOK: Anna Wintour OK" was scrawled across the top.

A humble threading salon stationed in the tunnel leading to the subway at Rockefeller Center blew up that article onto foam board and displayed it in the window for close to ten years until they closed. The last time I walked by, it was still propped up in a dark, dusty corner in the empty storefront.

What *Vogue* offered that most magazines don't was the opportunity to include your first-person experience in a story. Having succeeded in telling the world about my mustache, I was more than thrilled to take on another first-person assignment: writing about dermatologist Nicholas Perricone's salmon diet. A food story, at last! Dr. Perricone was unveiling a line of products, along with a prescription diet that he claimed reduced inflammation and made your skin glow. Amy told me to try it and report my findings. No one in the editorial meeting thought to give the story to a writer past the age of thirty, perhaps, who didn't still possess 90 percent of the collagen she'd been born with. And everyone assumed that eating salmon—and not much else—for three days would be an acceptable task. I didn't dare give up the assignment, but even the smell of salmon turned my stomach. "I am not sure I can do this for three days," I said to my sympathetic roommate, Catherine, later that night. "And the rest of the menu is mostly almonds."

The worst part of Dr. Perricone's regimen was that the salmon was supposed to be plain, just olive oil and lemon. I couldn't smother it in barbecue sauce or chase it with a sleeve of Oreos. My parents happened to be visiting during this story debacle, and we had reservations at a new Italian restaurant in the Flatiron District. I can still hear my deflated, sad voice asking the server if the chef would mind making me a simple roasted salmon filet. My dad kept waving forkfuls of tiramisu in my face, laughing. At the end of three days, I looked exactly the same, only defeated and hungry. "I don't know. Your skin looks kind of bright?" Catherine offered. I asked a few friends at work. "Tell me my skin looks glowing," I said. "Your skin looks glowing," they said. I wrote the story as honestly as I could, full of hopeful generalizations. It ran alongside an Irving Penn photograph of a slick slab of raw salmon sitting alone on a white plate. To this day, I can't stomach that fish. I eat oysters and escargot and have sucked Cheeto dust off of my toddler's fingers without batting an eye. Salmon is the one food that everyone I know seems to enjoy, and I'd rather swallow my Apple Watch band right now.

Here are a few things I took away from working at *Vogue*:

- During my time in the beauty department, everyone only painted their toenails in a nude or pale ballerina-pink polish, because that's what Anna did. She found colors garish, I heard. I followed suit. At first it seemed nuts, but I'm here to tell you that I am still painting my toenails nude twenty years later. Nude colors grow out almost invisibly and chips aren't noticeable, so your pedicure lasts longer and the polish doesn't stain your nail beds.

- If you were a savvy shopper—I was not (see: I'd rather nap in the deserted ladies' lounge at Lord & Taylor)—you could cobble together outfits that looked designer, even if they weren't. On one of my first days at the magazine, I complimented my coworker Rebecca's jacket. Rebecca was Amy Astley's assistant, and she sat in the cubicle in front of mine, so I stared at her back all day. "Oh, it's Old Navy," she whispered. "But it's an amazing copy of the new Marc by Marc." The only words I understood in that sentence were *Old* and *Navy*. But I learned that Marc by Marc was the lower (ha!) priced line of casualwear by Marc Jacobs, and Old Navy had succeeded in knocking off a cotton, cropped military jacket from the line that every underpaid editor at a fashion magazine owned. I didn't, because I wasn't fast enough. It sold out in every Old Navy within subway distance of my apartment.

• There were also editors who maxed out their credit cards buying the same designers Anna wore in an attempt to get her attention. I still, to this day, have never gotten over hearing that one editor I worked with was tens of thousands of dollars in debt, mostly from Prada.

• If you showed up to meetings prepared and spoke with confidence, Anna would treat you with respect, even if she didn't like your story idea.

After a little less than two years, I left *Vogue*. I didn't have another job. I went freelance, a move that looks incredibly stupid in today's world, as so many of the great magazines are shutting their doors and we all want good writing on the internet to be freeeeee even though there is a writer behind it who has to buy toilet paper. In 2002, though, magazines were still fat cats with lots of work to hand out. Amy Astley had moved to another floor to launch *Teen Vogue*, and I couldn't discern a path out of the beauty department into food or travel. I figured that going freelance would allow me to diversify. One incident spurred me on, and the more years that pass, the larger it looms. It is one of the few stories I look back on where I have a higher view of myself than I did at the time. That doesn't happen often. Usually I look back and marvel that I had friends or did not get arrested. This time my gut spoke wisely, and I listened. And it solidified a change in me that's been useful ever since.

I was sitting in an editorial meeting one afternoon, discussing the annual Age Issue. In the Age Issue *Vogue* ran pages and pages of real women—one from every decade of life, from twenties on up—wearing expensive clothes. I believe we capped it at seventy. The real women were, of course, artists and philanthropists and otherwise extremely fancy, wealthy, thin women—a gross, foregone conclusion all of us swallowed without debate. As we got to the sixties, each decade becoming harder and harder to cast, Laurie Jones pulled out a photo of a woman with an attached news article. She mentioned the woman's name and occupation. The woman was the CEO of a company. "She's Southern," Laurie (also Southern!) said. "But, you know, polished." Her tone was apologetic.

But, you know, polished.

What did that mean? No discernible accent? Living in New York City instead of Texas or Tennessee or Alabama? Nude toes?[1] What did it take to be part of the cool club, exactly? And had I made it? Was I not living here? Were my toes not nude? And then something inside snapped. It wasn't a sense of *I'll never be part of the cool club*. I was intuitive enough to know that even the socialites who got their jobs in the fashion department because they were children of New York royalty didn't feel like they were part of the cool club. Everyone is insecure and all that. No, it was that I knew I probably could be successful at *Vogue* if I wanted to; I'd just have to discard a comfortable part of me and leave it outside the building.

---

1.   All of those things, I believe, plus being super, super rich.

Which, in some instances, you need to do, maybe for a limited amount of time, and that's fine.

There were other Southerners sitting in that editorial meeting who didn't flinch. André Leon Talley was from North Carolina and did not fit any sort of mold, thank goodness, and he hung on for decades. Julia Reed seemed to get away with being unapologetically Mississippian, but that may have been because she was not technically on staff and only came into the office a couple of times a year. I can only speak for myself; after that meeting I thought, *I can't take off enough parts of me to fit in*. It wasn't purely the Southern thing. I didn't like to shop. I had no desire to vacation in the Azores. I didn't know where the Azores were. I wanted to wear clogs. (Note: this was before all the colorful Swedish clogs—or, even better, clogs that were Birkenstocks!—became fashionable again after designers started sending them down the runway during Fashion Week. No one at *Vogue* was wearing clogs or Birkenstocks in 2002.) This may be unpopular, but I do think there's a time and a place to button up and be respectful and try to learn something, within reason. I was young, my rights were not being violated in any way, so I let that meeting wash over me, I didn't say anything, and a few months later I told them I was leaving.

Everyone's math is different when it comes to how much you are willing to change or cover up to fit in, whether it's at a job or a garden club. There was nothing particularly noble about my leaving *Vogue*. The math ceased to add up after a while, is all. What I have come to learn in the years since is that there are situations and relationships in which you cannot avoid reshaping whole chunks of yourself. A job doesn't need to be one of them. To stay in a marriage, or even in some friendships, you will let go of things you think are important. Those sacrifices are worth it. Nothing was worth having my soul sucked out of my imitation Jimmy Choo heels every morning at *Vogue*. I'm so glad I worked there, I really am. And I'm so glad I moved on. Every cool club you want to be in is never as great as you think it will be.

A couple of years later, I did get to write about food, for a new website called The Kitchn. From that staff, I learned more about hospitality and serving others around the table than anywhere else, maybe even church. We wrote about "cooking by feel," which simply meant that the ultimate freedom in the kitchen came from learning enough basic rules and ingredient pairings to be able to cook without a recipe, to be flexible, to sense when something was finished, to pull together an easy meal with what's seasonal or on hand. Writing is a bit like that, in a way. You study great writers and listen to your editors and learn everything you can from every job, good or bad, so that, eventually, you know how to bend the rules to find your own voice. You feel your way.

Chapter 5

I'LL ALWAYS HAVE ARKANSAS

DURING THE SUMMER OF 1987, ON OUR FAMILY'S ANNUAL TRIP to Greers Ferry Lake in central Arkansas, my father ran over me with our station wagon. I wasn't critically injured, but it was close. The tires of the station wagon missed my head by about six inches.

I assume it was an accident. Of course it was. As stubborn and tiresome as I was as a rising fifth grader, I'm certain my father wasn't *actually* trying to kill me. That said, I never asked him. The incident happened, a narrative formed, we all agreed on the narrative, and then we never talked about it. Now, when I think I'd like to ask my dad about that day and, more importantly, how he must have felt pulling his child out from under a car after (allegedly, accidentally) running her over, I can't because he's dead. In the final few years of his life, it seemed like poor taste to bring it up.

My family's vacations to Greers Ferry are some of my favorite childhood memories, station wagon situations notwithstanding. When people get into discussions at dinner parties about beaches versus mountains, I say that I choose lakes, which many folks in the Northeast, where I now live, assume means mountains. They kind of go together up here. In this part of the country, lakes are frequently tucked between two peaks, like a swimming hole you reach on a hike in Acadia National Park or surrounded by the Adirondacks. Lakes in the North are cold and clear and beautiful. That's not what I'm talking about.

Lakes in the South can be surrounded by nothing but flat fields and are the temperature of urine, which thrills me to no end. I'd like every body of water I wade into from now until my death to be just slightly lower than a simmer. For a time my mother's parents owned a small cabin on Lake Mohawk in Mississippi. When you touched the bottom, a soft, silty mud would rise in between your toes, and you'd thank the Lord that the water was a foggy brown, because otherwise you'd see too many water moccasins to enjoy yourself. Mohawk was such a small lake that when we wanted to water-ski, we had to drive the boat in a constant circle, bumping over our own wake until it became too choppy to keep going. Greers Ferry is huge and deep, the result of a dam built around 1960 on the Little Red River. The floor is rocky, and the water is clear, shining deep emerald green when the light hits it. And yet it is still warm, at least when we went. My sister and I used to play a game where one of us would push the other underwater—while wearing life jackets—then stand on the shoulders of the underwater sibling and extend our legs, shoving the dunkee way, way down. When we popped up like a buoy a few seconds later, we'd report whether we went far enough to hit "the cold part" with our toes.

My dad loved both types of skiing—snow and water. He learned to snow-ski in college at the University of Michigan, and he learned to water-ski behind a houseboat back home in Memphis on the Mississippi River. He never liked the beach. He burned easily, and, as he said, there was nothing to do. So our family trips were almost always to the mountains or the lake (separate destinations, remember). When we went to Destin on the Florida panhandle, my mother drove us with some of her friends, and we left my dad at home. My sister and I burned easily, too, so in the pictures from those trips, when all the children would line up on the shoreline, Holland and I were the ones in wet cotton T-shirts and visors, while the other girls had on bikinis.

We ended up at Greers Ferry because my mother's brother Max lived in Little Rock, and his wife, Patti, was a water-skier. Her father, whom we called Boatman, for obvious reasons, owned a boat and introduced all of us to the sport. After the first couple of trips, my dad bought a ski boat that he parked in our driveway in the off-season. It was a pain to clean at the start of summer—Holland and I would barter chores to try to get out of scrubbing mildew off the seats—but the weatherproof cover made it an excellent hiding spot when necessary. Years ago one of the Boston Marathon bombers was found hiding in someone's boat in a quiet neighborhood not far from the city center. When I heard that, I had a vivid memory of the feeling of squeezing under the tight, canvas cover and letting it snap back as you fell inside. I'm sure it was pretty cozy, for what it's worth.

The first time I skied, I was probably five or six. My dad, even though he could slalom, put on two skis and held me in between his arms, with my bare feet resting just above his neoprene booted ones. When the boat pulled him up, he cradled me with his torso until I was able to stand—barely—on the tops of his skis: my legs splayed out, my hands holding on to my dad's forearms, trying not to slide off into the water rushing underneath us. The next summer I learned to ski on my own, as did my sister and my older cousin Jimbo. Patti taught all of us. My dad drove the boat.

The funniest detail about Patti is that she cannot swim. As she would tell you, her skill on skis—and she is an incredible skier— does not, for some reason, translate to moving her arms and legs in a coordinated motion that would keep her alive without a life jacket on. She's now in her sixties, and she will ride in a boat all day and float in the lake wearing her life jacket like a diaper, but she will not swim. Which makes it all the more remarkable that she bobbed in the water for hours on end trying to get the rest of us up on skis. We started early, around 5:30 or 6 a.m. "Time for ski camp," Patti would say as she squeezed our shoulders and told us to get out of bed. "The water is like glass. Let's get going."

She was right. If you wanted to have the best possible conditions for learning to ski, you wanted the least possible boats on the lake. I will say, those mornings are the only time I remember Greers Ferry feeling a touch chilly. I never wanted to go first, which meant you waded out from the shore and waited in the shallow water to be pulled out. I preferred to jump into the deeper parts of the lake, straight from the boat. But I didn't always get a choice. Holland, Jimbo, and I took turns. Patti would help us get our skis on and hold us in a sitting position, repeating the mantras we all knew: Sit like you're in a chair, keep your arms straight, and let the boat pull you up. When the boat had pulled all the slack out of the rope and started to slowly drag us, Patti would help us stay in position, and once we were steady for more than half a second, she'd yell, "Hit it!" and my dad would throw the boat into high gear.

When you are seven, it is pretty easy to get up on two skis. I'm not bragging. It just is. You weigh so little, you pop right up, and if you can remember not to bend your arms or lean forward, you are mostly golden. That part of learning to ski wasn't bad. Ski camp became tougher, however, when Patti decided it was time for all of us to learn how to slalom. She and my dad used the drop-a-ski method, which I'm not sure is still in vogue. But in the mid-1980s you got up on two skis and, when you felt ready and preferably were passing close by your rental house, you slipped your foot out of one ski and slipped it in the slot behind your other foot on the slalom ski. After you'd had a good run, you'd drive the boat around looking for the dropped ski in the brush along the shore. Sometimes my grandfather would have found it in front of the house where he was sitting on the porch watching us go by. That's if we were lucky. We lost a few too. Eventually, when we were comfortable with being in motion on one ski, Patti would declare it was time to get up on one from the start. On those mornings, we held on for dear life while our single ski wiggled back and forth and our weight, however insignificant, dragged behind the boat. We pressed our back foot into the ski to steady ourselves, but more often than not, in the early days, we would be blinded by the spray or fly forward, our faces skidding across the surface. We swallowed so much lake water that we could still feel it sloshing in our stomachs at night when we went to bed.

Ski camp ended in time for breakfast. We would come inside the house, where my mother and grandmother and other aunt, Mary Frances, had made biscuits and sausage and cheese grits, and we'd eat and take a nap before heading out again. If the lake was crowded and the water was choppy, we'd go tubing. But back then it wasn't like it is now with tubing. I see pictures of friends' kids these days, and the kids are sitting upright in an inflatable living room set. I swear there are seat belts, and some of these contraptions fit ten to fifteen children. You half expect a waiter to come by with a tray of pigs in a blanket from somewhere outside the wake. In my day, tubes were one step up from a bicycle tire, and if your cousins were driving the boat, there was a high likelihood you would break your clavicle. At the end of the day, we would play Trivial Pursuit and pool. The house we rented for most of the years I can remember was called Shandolin, and everything about it, from the posh name to the brown-and-white Tudor timbering on the facade, was out of place in Arkansas. I once visited the building that housed my husband's fraternity at Harvard (only they call them Finals Clubs because they're pretentious), and this rental house was a close approximation—lots of leather Chesterfield sofas and a wood-paneled game room. I learned to play pool during those years. Not well, but well enough that I can put backspin on the cue ball and shoot fairly accurately with one foot on the floor and one butt cheek on the edge of the table. My mother's older brother, Jimmy, would make Velvet Hammers—extremely alcoholic vanilla milk shakes—for the adults, and we could hear him laughing while he smoked on the outside deck as we fell asleep.

Shandolin was booked the week we wanted it in 1987. We had to stay at another house down the road, which was owned by Gil Gerard, the actor who played Buck Rogers. Gil grew up in Little Rock. I never watched Buck Rogers, and I don't remember anything about that house. After the station wagon accident, we went back to Shandolin until we got older and no longer went to Greers Ferry at all.

It was the final day of our trip, which meant that it was time to get the boat out of the water. During the week our boat trailer sat in an empty grass lot near the loading ramp. When it was time to go home, we had to rehitch the trailer to the back of our car, then back the trailer into the lake on the ramp, get the boat on the trailer, secure everything, and then pack the boat with all of the life jackets and coolers and other bulky items that wouldn't fit in the back of the station wagon. Dad needed someone to help him hitch the trailer to the car. I volunteered to go. I'd done this job countless times, even though I was only ten years old. It wasn't that hard. I stood by the trailer hitch while Dad backed up the car, shouting through the open back window whether he needed to move to the right or the left to line up the tennis-ball-shaped hitch on the bumper with the corresponding part on the boat trailer.

That day I was straddling the front end of the trailer, where it narrowed to a point. A metal pole with notches on it, which allowed you to adjust the height of the trailer with a crank, was right in front of me. It came up to my waist. I put both of my hands up, palms forward, ready to give my dad directions—a little to the left, keep coming, okay, stop. The back window, the one that you looked out of from the backward-facing seat in all 1980s station wagons, was rolled down. The car began moving slowly toward me, then I saw my dad turn his head and look back at me, draping his right arm over the back of the passenger-side front seat. At that point the car engine went from a hum to a growl, and the back bumper started accelerating toward me and the trailer. I opened my mouth to say, "That's too fast!" but I didn't get the chance. I felt my face slam into the ground, dry grass crackling in my right ear, and then I heard the roar of the car come over me. When it stopped, I could tell that the station wagon's four tires had straddled my body by a hair. My back, inches below the car's hot, greasy undercarriage, was unscathed. I was small enough that the car had just moved over me like a turtle shell. I did not dare move.

Immediately I could hear my dad screaming my name. I have a memory from that morning, and I can't remember if it is something I thought later on or something I heard my mother or my aunts or uncles say, but how terrified must my dad have been? Having to get out of the car, knowing his daughter was underneath it, and not knowing what he was going to find when he pulled me out. I think about that all the time. I screamed back and reached my hands into the light on the other side of the tires. My dad grabbed my hands and dragged me sideways and upright in one swift tug. I was able to walk to the passenger door and sit down; it was only once I was inside the car that I realized my left knee was badly cut, straight across the kneecap, and I had a hole in my lower abdomen, just above my right hip bone. The tall metal pole that was in front of me on the trailer had gouged my side before I was thrown off my feet.

Dad drove back to the Buck Rogers house, left me in the car, and ran inside. Within seconds he transferred me to the back seat of my uncle Max's car, with my legs over my mother's lap. Max was known to drive like a bat out of hell, and the closest hospital was at least forty-five minutes away. On the way I made a joke about his driving so fast that the bumps in the road were making every-thing hurt worse. He laughed and said it was a good sign I still had a sense of humor. But when I looked at the hole in my side, I could see some contents of my body I was sure were not supposed to be exposed: greenish, worm-like things that bobbed up and down through the opening in my skin.

At the hospital they stitched me up. It took a while. My body, from neck to knee, was dyed mustard yellow from iodine swabs. But, miraculously, no bones were broken. I healed. I still have two faint white scars—on my left knee and lower right abdomen. In both, you can still see the crosshatches where the stitches were. As far as childhood accidents or illnesses go, it was nothing. I have more serious lingering issues from cavities. But it was also weird. Everyone in my family said "the car malfunctioned." I said to my friends, "The car malfunctioned. When my dad pressed the gas pedal lightly, it got stuck, and the car zoomed back." Did an adult in my life say those exact words? I honestly don't remember. No one corrected me, though. And I was young. And I'm sure my dad felt awful. Still. The station wagon disappeared (which wasn't strange—my dad was in the car business, so he would lease our cars to clients and bring home new ones all the time), and the story became a joke I'd trot out every few years. "Yeah, Dad, but then again, you did run me over with the family station wagon." He'd nod, I'd laugh, and I'd continue to believe the stupid car somehow malfunctioned. Everyone let me believe it.

This past summer I went back to Greers Ferry for the first time in close to thirty years. Our family vacations ended once Jimbo, Holland, and I became teenagers and went to college. Patti and Max, younger than my parents by more than a decade, had their own young children, and Patti's parents bought their own house at the lake. My parents visited Greers Ferry, staying with Patti and Max, a few times over the years, but my sister and I never managed to get there. We had busy young-adult lives, and then our own kids, and it was hard enough to get to Memphis to see our parents and friends. Adding on a trip to Arkansas never felt like a priority. And, of course, it wouldn't be the same anyway. Shandolin was off the rental market. My grandparents and uncle Jimmy had died. Family vacations do what they do, which is splinter into self-contained pods, clustered on your branch of the family tree. Jimbo and his family live in Houston. Patti and Max's three kids are currently in Arkansas, New Mexico, and Hawaii. This year, however, my family was going to be in Memphis for two weeks in August. My youngest cousin, Madeline, the one in New Mexico, mentioned to me that she and her family were planning to be at the lake, at her grandparents' house, for part of that time. I invited myself.

The water was just as clear and warm as I remembered—and, more importantly, had promised my children, who had declared that my lake couldn't possibly be as beautiful as the lake at their summer camp in New Hampshire, which is gorgeous, yes, but chilly and filled with weak New England tubers. The first morning we were there, I got in the water with my two older children, holding them steady, saying, "Sit like you're in a chair, keep your arms straight, and let the boat pull you up." I swam toward them every time they succumbed to the spray instead of standing up, backstroked to grab the rope handle as the boat came around, held them again, taught them to yell "Hit it!" when they felt ready. Eventually both of them got up, confidently, and skied for so long that I could barely see the boat anymore as I floated in the open water, happily left behind. I got up on one ski on my first try, which was a miracle and made me feel like a goddess, if only because it is one of the only ways I can still outperform my children. Like female mayflies, who rise from their watery beginnings in streambeds to live in flight for only five minutes, I emerge from the spray to skim and dart across the wake for a few glorious minutes, then fling the rope and sink, half-dead.

I missed growing up with Patti and Max's three kids, because they were much younger than I was, but there they were: driving the boat, jumping off rock cliffs with my kids, making stupendous tacos. The whole trip was a gift. There was even a pool table in the basement. And then one afternoon we began talking about the different houses we'd stayed in over the years. When the Buck Rogers house came up, I mentioned that that was the year my dad ran me over. "Oh, right, when he stepped on the gas instead of the brake," said Max.

Well. Of course.

I mean, I knew that's what had happened. As a parent I'd done the same thing many times, only I was always in park, so my car revved but didn't go anywhere. I'd turn to the back seat to pick up a dropped pacifier or hand a snack to a kid, and as I stretched my body out, I'd push off with my foot, occasionally pushing down on the gas instead of the brake. It's so easy to do. Of course that was the clear explanation. The station wagon did not malfunction. But when Max said it, my heart fell. I'd told myself something different for so long, and now my dad was gone, and I wasn't interested in revising any memories of him. He got rid of the car! He took the broken car story far enough to *get rid of our car*. Was it just to preserve my recollection of what happened? Did he want to show in some tangible way that I was still safe with him? I suppose it's possible he couldn't bear to drive that car anymore. Maybe he withheld the full truth because parents do that. If the kid is okay, if the kid has moved on, we let them. We swallow the unsavory details.

I have done some truly dumb things that endangered my kids' safety (please flip to chapter 9, where I detail losing my six-year-old in Times Square). I know how a moment of lapse, of grabbing your child just before he scooters off the curb and into oncoming traffic, eats away at you. I've found it's better to meditate on the moments

IT WAS AN UGLY COUCH ANYWAY

I held them steady, the times I cradled their wobbly, bent legs in a sitting position in the water, waiting for the moment they would stand. I hope my dad spent the years after 1987 remembering how when he pulled me out from under the car, I was whole. I hope he remembers the feeling of us skimming the lake together, my bare feet on his skis.

Chapter 6

WITH MY SINCEREST APOLOGIES TO THE LATE NORA EPHRON AND BASICALLY EVERY FEMALE WRITER I ADMIRE

IN 2006 NORA EPHRON WROTE A BOOK, *I FEEL BAD ABOUT MY NECK*, which is full of wonderful pieces about the complexities and indignities of being an older woman. It hit number one on the *New York Times* Nonfiction Best Sellers list. It is a superb book, as all of hers are, which I have to say because I am a female essayist living in New York City. I once wrote about having a crush on Harry Burns, a character she invented in *When Harry Met Sally*.

None of what I'm about to write is her fault.

Ephron was sixty-five years old when the book was published. I did not know her personally, and I never saw her neck, but I've seen my mother's, and most women in their sixties and seventies do, indeed, have "necks with wattles and necks with creases that are on the verge of becoming wattles," as Ephron writes. She claims the decline begins at age forty-three. Whereas women can employ Botox and laser and retinol to make the skin on their faces look younger, there's nothing that can be done about the neck, she explains. It's the giveaway.

Now, Ephron may have been the first—or at least the most famous—writer to talk about her neck, but she wasn't the last. Among a certain demographic (women like me, who write for a living and are north of forty-three, when our necks start to go), mentioning one's neck has become a shorthand, a cliché, to discussing anything about aging. In every piece there is a nod to Ephron's neck, then a turn to anything from crow's feet to mom jeans to how much the writer spends on her roots. Don't even get me started on the riffs on the title. Something similar happened after David Foster Wallace's essay "Consider the Lobster" ran in *Gourmet* in 2004. The story was such a supernova that it became headline canon, and food editors everywhere began titling *their* stories "Consider the Mushroom," "Consider the Waffle," "Consider the Lobster— Being Overfished." Things like that. Similarly, just in the past year I've seen essays by female writers titled "I Feel Great About My Neck" and "I Feel Better About My Neck." They were both lovely essays by writers I like. But if I am being honest, I'm starting to get annoyed by it all. The titles, the hand-wringing about injectables, the necks, everything related to how we look on the outside and what a missed opportunity it was not to appreciate our un-wattled, twenty-year-old selves. Where would we be if Nora Ephron had titled her book *I Feel Bad About the Hemorrhoids I'm Still Dealing with from Childbirth Five Years Ago*? Imagine the possibilities.

There are just so many other body parts and functions to explore. Last week my friend Stephanie went on a rant about the fact that at some point in your late thirties, according to her, the skin that covers your kneecaps begins swinging free like deflated balloons. Who knew? Stephanie claims it is most pronounced when doing a downward dog in yoga, which is why I haven't noticed a change in my knee skin; I don't like yoga. But I *have* been growing a patchy beard every day since high school, an affliction I would trade in a hot second for droopy kneecaps. When women I know talk about how they are going to sign a pact with a friend who will commit to "plucking that one curly chin hair" for them when they're old and incapacitated, I laugh and laugh. One chin hair? One? I'm going to need a small lawn mower, not tweezers, by that point. Is that interesting to anyone? Is everyone starting with necks because necks are more palatable? Is everything else too gross?

I hope not, because what I'd really love to discuss is peeing my pants.

Don't worry, this is also a story about running and family dynamics. But it starts with peeing my pants. My mother hates when I say the word *pee*. And I don't blame her. *Tinkle* or *tee tee*, her preferred choices, are both a little less crass sounding. But I am forty-six years old, and if I'm going to be real about the indignities of involuntarily wetting my pants, I think I need to come in with more firepower than *tinkle*.

Women my age pee their pants because of their children. Carrying a child during pregnancy and giving birth weakens our pelvic muscles to the point that urine leaks out when those muscles are put to the test—for example, when you sneeze. I used to think that the physical phenomenon of pushing a baby through the birth canal was what really messed things up, but I've known friends who had C-sections experience incontinence too. Simply the weight of the kid bearing down on your privates for nine months will do the trick. I've heard there are surgical options and physical therapy that can help, but neither is a sure thing. Back in 2017 Michael and I went to the fortieth birthday party of a couple, friends of his from college. The husband and wife threw themselves a joint party at a country club with a DJ who was clearly told to stick to a playlist of 1980s and '90s hits. When "Jump Around" by House of Pain came on and we all jumped like teenagers, women began discreetly peeling off to go to the bathroom. By the time I got to the ladies room, it was full. One woman had her dress hiked up, her leg on the sink ledge, and was dabbing between her thighs with a wad of paper towels.

"So, we are all just peeing our pants from jumping?" I asked.

"YES!" a chorus rang out.

"Isn't there a surgery that helps with this?" I said, laughing.

"I've had it. It didn't do anything," said one woman from inside a stall.

"Me too! Useless!" said another.

As we stood bemoaning our predicament, it became clear to me that nothing was going to help other than going back in time and remembering to do Kegel exercises, which no woman has ever remembered to do regularly, I'm sorry. For the rest of my life, I will have to stop walking and clench when I have to sneeze. Trampolines are off-limits for me. Ditto jumping rope. Eventually, I suspect, I will start wearing a maxi pad prophylactically, which I've heard is the end of the road, around the same time someone should start mowing my chin.

The one thing I am not going to give up on account of my incontinence is running. Which is an outrageous thing for me to say, because, on principle, I really hate to exercise. Growing up I was a ballet dancer. No one would argue that dancing is not exercise or does not require physical discipline. But it was always indoors—meaning I did not have to contend with the swamp air of the Deep South while exerting myself. And it included lots of downtime, when I might sew ribbons onto my pointe shoes, and it involved missing school to perform in *The Nutcracker* every December at the Orpheum Theater in downtown Memphis.

In high school I quit ballet to explore other options, like soccer and track, neither of which went well. I was decent at soccer but not great, and my career ended senior year when I was sideswiped by a defender on the other team who knocked my kneecap straight off its perch. When it happened, I looked down at my leg as I lay on the field, and there was just a soft, hollow indention where my knee had been; the cap was ninety degrees to the right, looking like I had a Double Stuf Oreo tucked under the skin. (If I do start to notice my knee skin getting loose, I'll just blame all the stretching and shifting that happened from this event.) During track preseason, when we were expected to run several miles in the neighborhood near our school to get in shape, my friend Murff and I would run to her house, which was close by, pick up some popcorn, and then have someone drive us back to school—dropping us far enough away that our coach wouldn't see—before jogging back to the track. That was a good indication of my level of commitment to running.

My dad loved to run. He liked to tell me about what it was like to run before companies made dedicated shoes for the sport. He also skied in leather lace-up boots strapped to wooden skis. Every time my sister or I would put on a new, lightweight sneaker or slip into a fiberglass ski boot, my dad would just shake his head in awe and appreciation. What a time to be alive! With entire Foot Lockers full of options!

Dad ran in the mornings, before I went to school, with two of his friends, Mr. Middlecoff and Mr. Watson. Mr. Middlecoff lived in our neighborhood, just down a hill and around the corner in a cul-de-sac, but Mr. Watson was several miles away, so they alternated running in our neighborhood with driving to Mr. Watson. I don't know how far they typically ran; none of them, as far as I remember, ever trained for a long race. My dad would run our school's 5K Turkey Trot—which was not, as many Turkey Trots are, on Thanksgiving Day. Our Turkey Trot was called a Turkey Trot because the mascot for my all-girls' school was the turkey. And before you go mocking me for having a turkey as a school mascot, please know that it was incessantly, exhaustively heralded as a *wild* turkey, the specific breed known for its cleverness at avoiding capture. Even so, every year, in the days leading up to Thanksgiving break, our headmaster dressed up as a turkey at morning chapel and pretended to get shot by a hungry hunter, and we all wailed dramatically. The Turkey Trot took place in April. I had multiple T-shirts commemorating the annual event, but I rarely ran in it. Instead, I would sit and cheer on my dad and older sister, who also loved to run and still does. My dad would cross the finish line and turn to me. "Next year, Elizabear! You'll run!" And I'd always say no.

The first time I remember running more than a mile was the summer before my freshman year of high school. I was supposed to be getting into shape for the upcoming soccer season. Certain that my running would be sporadic and short-lived, I convinced my parents to buy me some Nike cross-trainers, which I thought would be more versatile. They were designed for walking, maybe aerobics, and, given their heft, possibly hiking the Appalachian Trail. These shoes were shaped like loaves of bread and weighed as much as a Chihuahua. Running in them in the August heat in Memphis felt like clogging in a shallow pool of pudding. But I told myself that I wouldn't stop until I reached my friend Dhevi Kumar's house in the neighborhood just over from mine, which seemed like a reasonable goal. I barely made it.

Every time my feet smacked the pavement, it was as if suction cups sprouted on my soles to keep them there. There was no cloud cover. My breaths turned to wheezes. Dhevi's parents had these silk rugs in their formal living room that I knew from experience felt soft and cool, almost icy, when you ran your hands over them. As I slowly jogged the last few hundred yards, I imagined lying on those rugs, feeling the heat draining from my body. Later, when I had my mother drive the same route that I had run—in 1991, that's how you measured how far you'd gone, by punching the car's odometer to zero and clocking the distance—it was 1.21 miles. I will always remember that exact distance and how proud my dad was when he got home. For 1.21 miles. He thought it was the start of something.

What it started, however, was years of me running to please someone else. My dad desperately wanted me to run track. I ran track. Once or twice, I ran a 5K with him to make him happy. A couple of years after college, my sister invited me to run a half-marathon on Kiawah Island in South Carolina with her and her husband. Because I thought it would make me disciplined, and because I relished any chance to hang out with my older sister's friends, I said yes. I ran it twice, maybe even three times. I don't remember exactly, due to situational amnesia brought on by the fact that I hated every mile of training.

And thus began my slow slide into doing nothing as an adult, when it came to exercise. There was simply no motivation. I realize that many, many people say they feel better, sleep better, have better mental health. Those things are their motivation. Not mine. I have never felt a runner's high. Any sort of class, like yoga or spinning, makes me feel vulnerable and idiotic in front of strangers, which I think is bad for my mental health. Once I went to SoulCycle with my friend Katie, and for a week afterward, it felt like someone had taken a baseball bat to my undercarriage. Katie said, "It gets better as you take more classes." I said I'd be happy to meet her after class for a margarita the next time. Absolutely nothing was incentive enough for me to exercise regularly. Not cute workout clothes. Not meeting up with a friend at zero dark thirty "to keep me accountable." Not a reward Pop-Tart. I might go through a phase where I would run a few times a week for six months, but then I'd have a baby, or it would be a hot summer, or I didn't like my sports bras anymore, and I'd stop. For two or three years.

So it is very strange for me to say that I began to enjoy running at age forty-three, during a pandemic, right around the time I started peeing on myself every time I coughed. I know I really enjoy running because the steps I have to go through to get out the door are absurd. I am middle-aged, and what moisture is left in my body is being hoarded by my skin in its quest not to look like a dried riverbed. I get dehydrated easily. So I need to drink a lot of water in the hour or so before I run. But, of course, that makes me have to go to the bathroom, and once is never enough. I go five or six times before I walk out the door. A normal time, then several mini efforts, a drop here, a drop there, like I'm squeezing an old lime.

If there is so much as a whisper of urine in my body, it breaks free, and it leaves the door cracked for its friends.

The reason I endure the discomfort of wet leggings is that I have realized something very important about running. My children do not do it. That's how this whole enterprise started. So many of my daily acts are things my children would very much like to do with me. Make pancakes? They'll help. Sit on my bed and read? Suddenly my bed looks more cozy than the couch they were happily sitting on just five seconds before. Take a shower? The toddler is already shimmying out of his shorts. But run? No takers. During the first few months of the pandemic, when all five of us were stuck at home, going for a run was the only option for getting away from everyone. I just wanted to be alone, and there was absolutely nowhere in a two-bedroom apartment for that to happen. I had to leave the house. If I was going to leave the house, I figured I might as well make it productive. Another detail: I was frequently blowing my top around 4 or 5 p.m., and I thought running might loosen some of the rage. I began running about an hour before I needed to start making dinner. The idea was that I would come back with just enough of a renewed spirit to make it to bedtime without strangling anyone. Is that what people mean when they say exercise is helpful for your mental health? I get it now.

Any time I begin running after a long hiatus, it's predictably terrible. Before this current streak, I'd last run regularly before getting pregnant with Sam. That was 2017. Starting out, I took it slow. Our apartment is on Central Park West, so I only had to cross the street to get into the park, and we are about eight blocks north of the Jacqueline Kennedy Onassis Reservoir, a body of water with a groomed running path and beautiful wrought-iron fence around it. One loop is 1.6 miles. Slowly, I worked my way up from two miles to three to occasionally four. That's the thing about running. No one cares how far I go. Sometimes I think I'd like to be able to easily run five or six miles, but I probably won't. And unlike a group class or, heaven forbid, one of those circuit workout places where you compete with your name and time up on a whiteboard for everyone to see, there's no one checking.

I also do not feel bad about refusing to run with friends. My sister runs with her friend Olivia. My dad ran with Mr. Middlecoff and Mr. Watson. When my dad, who was the oldest of the three, could no longer run, they walked. When he was in his seventies, dealing with the early effects of Parkinson's, and could no longer walk long distances, he and Mr. Middlecoff shifted to simply sitting and eating their favorite smoked chicken wings at a spartan take-out restaurant in a strip mall near the airport. I understand plenty of people like company. But not me. One day last winter, I ran into my friend Patricia as I was starting out on a run. She was on a walk in the North Woods of Central Park with her family. "Oh, you're going for a run? I'll join you!" she said. Which, first of all, what kind of person is just ready to run on a moment's notice? Had she even gone to the bathroom recently? She was wearing entirely too many layers—a long-sleeved fleece, a puffy vest, *and* a beanie—and yet she went four miles without so much as breathing heavily. I was stunned at her audacity, inviting herself like that, and I told her so. But in hindsight, I realized she deserved a pass. Her alternative was a walk with her husband and four kids. She saw an escape. I understood. I was doing the same thing.

I've learned my lesson since. When a friend asks if I'd like to run together, I say no. That it is my only time alone. That I selfishly protect it. That I'm prone to wetting my pants, and they might be ashamed to be seen with me. Even my husband knows that on the occasions we head out to run at the same time, he should take the paved road that loops around the park while I run the reservoir. Or, if I decide to run the loop, he should go in a different direction. If I see someone I know while I'm running, I wave and smile but do not stop.

The pandemic and the way it compressed my family around me in an ever-claustrophobic vise made me realize how much I craved being alone. I started to remember how many times I'd read in the Bible that Jesus went off on his own, even when there were crowds of people and needy disciples begging for his attention. He pushed the boat away from the shore or went into the wilderness. Luke 5:16 reads: "Jesus often withdrew to lonely places and prayed." I am an enthusiastic extrovert, and yet nothing sounded more wonderful to me than to withdraw to a lonely place. I began to listen to worship music while I ran. I turned the volume up so loud that I couldn't hear myself breathing heavily or my shoes scraping the gravel of the reservoir path. Some days it was old-school Amy Grant and Twila Paris; some days I would run to a playlist from a megachurch with a rock band. All I wanted was to hear God's promises sung over me. I was wrung out, parched, brittle, but he was good, present, forgiving. He could breathe life into a valley of dry bones.

The crazy thing about my quest to be alone while running is that I was running in New York City, where no one is ever really alone. Even in the months of strict lockdown, the parks were open, and we all needed a break from our apartments. First we ran with masks pulled down around our chins. We would pull them up if the path was bottlenecked and we needed to run close by someone for a few paces. As the weather got warmer, we ran with our masks wrapped around our upper arms—there in case, but out of the way. They were like little folded flags waving from triceps.

Most of the time, in any part of Central Park, you see tourists. Pedicabs are full of them, as are the horse-drawn carriages that get in your way as you round the south end of the loop. Tourist traffic is especially heavy around the reservoir on the weekends. You will be running and see a couple standing with their backs to the iron fence, perched on the edge of the stone ledge that rings the reservoir, while a friend stands across the path, trying to take a picture. Some runners slow down and jog in place for a second before they cross in front of the camera. Others plow right through. There are days when it happens four or five times on one trip around.

During the pandemic, though, there were no tourists. I couldn't know for sure, but I assumed everyone running in the park lived in Manhattan, probably uptown, maybe even in my immediate neighborhood. It was just us, the residents. And we tended to each other in small ways. We nodded and smiled if we caught someone's eye. We gave each other wide berths in the early days. We stopped and clapped if we happened to be running at 7 p.m., when the city cheered for health-care workers, the sound beginning in the buildings at the edge of the park and rolling through the trees until it reached us. It was not easy to be in the city at times, and I wanted to fist-bump every runner I passed. "Look! We are still here! Look how many of us there are, still here, still looking out for one another."

My dad never went for a run in New York City, but he would have loved it. He loved so much about the city: the subway system, especially, and pizza from Mama's Pizzeria on 106th Street and Amsterdam Avenue, where he once, thrillingly, saw a crew filming an episode of *Law & Order*. By the time I moved to New York after college, he was in his early sixties, and while he was still in great shape, he was no longer jogging. We had so many other things to do. I wonder all the time that if I had just been a more willing partner, we would have jogged around the reservoir together a few times, before he got older and slower and stopped running altogether. He would have loved rounding the northeast corner at sunset and looking back to see the buildings in Midtown light up. I hate that we never got to share that, but I think of him with every mile.

A lot of things in my life are better in my forties. Maybe exercise is one of them. Maybe I couldn't appreciate the sacredness of being alone, even if it involved shin splints, until I had three kids. Maybe I couldn't keep going until I had a pack of stranger-neighbors trucking alongside me. Maybe I needed the city lights. Or the slight humiliation of peeing my pants to remind me that my body is capable of so much, but it still leaks—pee, tears, swear words—because I'm still human. I take great pride in the fact that it is imperfect and slowly descending back to the dust, but it carries me home, where my family and a change of pants are waiting.

Chapter 7

LIKE WE OWN THE PLACE

Moving: Part 2

AFTER MY FIRST PHONE CALL WITH LOIS, THE TWO OF US ENTERED into a riveting pattern, where I would call and talk to her about selling us the apartment and she would tell me that she was definitely going to, she just needed to get in touch with her lawyer, and to call her back in two weeks. It was spring when we began this dance. Late March turned into April and April turned into May. New York warmed up, and I would often walk from our apartment across the park to the New York Society Library on Seventy-Ninth Street and Madison Avenue, where I write. We both meandered, I through the paths running along the Great Lawn toward the East Side, Lois through the details of her life and various reasons she hadn't called me back yet.

Lois had no voicemail, no texting, and no email. But in all the times I have called her, she's picked up every time but twice.

She knows it's me. She's always happy to hear from me. She never seems annoyed.

Lois starts talking before I can even say, "Hi! How are you?" into the tips of my AirPods. Sometimes, when she sounds like she's been napping or maybe just woke up, her voice has a drawl that's almost Southern. The word *lawyer* comes out "lar-yer." I picture my Mississippi grandmother on the other end, the one who is long dead, and I feel about Lois the way I felt about her when I'd call from New York in the first few months I lived here: protective, apologetic, that I needed to speak up. But Lois is not from Mississippi. She's from Harlem. Over the course of a few months, I get snippets of her life: how she was one of six children, that she worked for the US Postal Service at one point, how she was married twice, once to a man who lived in our neighborhood, which was how she ended up being a patient of the doctor who worked out of our building and who ended up becoming her second husband. The doctor was from Egypt. Lois saw the pyramids! He loved her daughter as if she was his own. He once sent her daughter on a trip around Italy for her birthday. Lois brought it up several times, that trip to Italy.

"My accountant, he's a good man. He did work for my husband for years. He said he's going to find me the name of a lawyer," she said one April morning. I had gathered that Lois's late husband had owned several apartments as investment properties. She'd sold a few in the building where she currently lived in tight, private deals, without paying a real estate agent, and she was determined to do the same here. Michael and I were all for it. If a real estate agent got involved, who knows what would happen. He might convince Lois to clean it out, renovate it, put it on the market, and incite a bidding war. Our hope was to offer her a fair price that left us enough money to renovate and saved her the hassle and expense of paying an agent and clearing out all the junk. We'd take it as is.

That's all she wanted, Lois would say. "Some people tell me I should empty the apartment and sell it. Nah! I don't want to deal with all that!" And then, a few weeks later, on a day when she seemed tired or upset, she'd say, "There are some lamps that I might want. Maybe I should call a real estate agent I know." One week she would complain that she'd paid three months of maintenance and wanted to be rid of that expense "by the end of the year!" The next, she'd casually mention that paying the maintenance was no big deal. But then every conversation would end the same way:

"We have the same goal. You want the apartment, and I want you to have it."

Or, "We are two strong women. We will get this done!"

Or, "I told my accountant that I want to see children running around in the apartment. Your family is going to have it."

Or, "I don't care how much money I make. I just want you to take the apartment."

And then: "Call me back in two weeks."

Michael has told me that I'm not a great judge of character. He thinks I assume too many people are trustworthy and fun and have good intentions. I think he's half right. Am I naive or gullible? Maybe, occasionally, if someone is skeezy but has a very good sense of humor. But really what I'm usually thinking when a faint alarm bell starts going off about someone is that, if you just give me time, if I can just talk to someone long enough, I'll figure them out. I always feel like I have the upper hand, like I can outsmart people. With Lois, though, I was sure—am sure, still—that she truly wanted nothing more than to sell us her apartment for a reasonable price that satisfied everyone's needs. Despite the stalling and the incongruous statements, I was sure. Every time I called, she'd say talking to me made her feel better, even when her blood pressure was high. She apologized over and over for how long this was taking, for the stress it was putting on my family. I said that it was fine. It was fine! We want you to feel comfortable, I said. We want to make this easy for you, I said. Would we take pictures of the renovated apartment and let her see them when it was all finished? she asked. Pictures? I laughed. You'll come over for dinner! You can spend the night! I said. Lois started crying. She was so happy we were going to buy it.

All of the dawdling about details and finding a lawyer was simply part of dealing with an eighty-one-year-old woman who did not own a smartphone, I told myself. What else could it be?

Michael and I moved ahead. We wanted to put an offer in writing to Lois. But in order to know how much we could pay for the apartment, we needed a ballpark on the renovation. Jeff, our building manager, knew one contractor who was already working on another apartment on a higher floor and agreed to walk through with us. A friend of mine offered another contractor, a second opinion, who came a few days later. What we got were vastly different numbers, although the second guy was clearly very high-end. He kept saying things like, "Well, if you move that wall, you'll just end up taking down all the walls, trust me." And, "Once you have to patch the floor in the kitchen, you'll just want to rip up all of the original flooring and start from scratch, trust me." I didn't trust him. We understood that unforeseen expenses would come up, but we also knew we were going to have to work within some boundaries and financial constraints. "But I don't want to take down all the walls. I like the layout," I said to the second contractor. "Eh. You're gonna take down all the walls," he said. We decided to split the difference between the two estimates, researched comps in the neighborhood, and came up with a price we felt was a little low but gave us room for negotiation. Plus, it factored in paying for junk removal, which we would be taking on. Who knew what we'd find when we started excavating?

A few important things were happening while we did all of this research. Because we needed to get the lay of the land and take contractors through the apartment, we started borrowing the key to the apartment from our doormen and letting ourselves in pretty frequently. We had Lois's permission. It wasn't like we were breaking and entering. But soon the dark, cluttered rooms began to feel like *ours*. Here was the boys' room. Here was the dining room. Here's your closet. Here's mine. We'll definitely restore those old cast-iron windows. I like the crooked hallway that leads to the master bath, don't you?

It felt like we already owned it. We had two architects walk through. We paid one to give us some preliminary plans—we didn't want to do much, just make one bathroom a little bigger, open up some small doorways, push part of the kitchen out a couple of feet. This architect was kind and soft-spoken, slight—a feature I could only think would be helpful as he weaved through the piles of furniture with his laser tape measure, trying to get an accurate floor plan down. Did we have a wish list? He wanted to know. Inspiration images? Michael and I had been homeowners since 2008, and I had hung light fixtures and painted furniture. But we'd never done any type of construction, never knocked down a wall or refaced kitchen cabinets. People say things like, "It's nice to buy a fixer-upper so you can make it your own. You can put your stamp on it," and I've always rolled my eyes—because, honestly, most people's stamps look remarkably the same—but suddenly all I wanted in my life was to pick out a kitchen faucet and shop for bathroom tile. I looked around our current apartment and realized how much we'd just accepted, all of those builder-grade finishes, because we were young and barely able to pay the mortgage. We wallpapered a bathroom, then a closet. The boob lights had remained, however. So did the cheap cabinet knobs. And yet here we were in our mid-forties. Julia would be leaving for college in eight years. All at once I saw every five-bedroom house in Memphis that some high school friend had renovated and decorated, every farmhouse in Charlottesville that a New Yorker had restored (for a fraction of the cost of their two-bedroom in Manhattan!), even every apartment in the city that a couple older or richer than we were had bought and combined with the apartment next door (the dream), and I wanted my piece. I was a grown-up, wasn't I? Hadn't I been a good soldier, paying my dues in a two-bedroom with three children? I was owed this, I reasoned. Ignoring the unfortunate truth in life that we are not rewarded for our emotional maturity or patience with material goods, I settled on the belief that Lois was right. This apartment was meant to be ours. We were all on the same page.

Our lawyer drew up a contract with our offer for the apartment. It was June. We had an accepted offer on our current apartment, having put it on the market during our late-spring burst of optimism that everything with Lois would move like butter around a hot skillet. Lois, meanwhile, had found a lawyer but refused to give us his name. "It's okay. I've called him. I'm just waiting for him to get back to me," she'd say. So I wrote her a letter outlining our offer and mailed it to her, along with a copy of the contract and several color photos of the inside of the apartment, just in case her lawyer wasn't aware of its condition. When she received it, she called. "Oh, thank you. Thank you. Now I just need to Xerox this somewhere, and then I can take copies to my accountant and my lawyer," she said. "Call me back in two weeks."

"Lois, wait." I paused to make sure she hadn't already hung up. I had heard the word *Xerox* and imagined Lois wandering the streets looking for a Kinko's. "You know, Lois, we could email copies of the contract to your lawyer and your accountant for you, if you want. Would that be helpful?" I asked.

"You can? Oh, yes, please do that," she said. And she gave me their names and phone numbers. I wrote them down, looked them up online, got their email addresses. Sometimes it was like that. Stonewalling for weeks and then a switch flipped. Open road.

Now we had the name of her accountant and lawyer. Our lawyer emailed both a copy of the contract, with photos of the place, and an explanation that I had been talking to Lois for months, and we had discussed the price already. We clearly explained that we lived in the same building, that Michael was on our co-op board, that our offer reflected the fact that Lois would be saving a huge amount of money and time by not clearing out and renovating the apartment herself. This could be quick and easy, as soon as she signed the contract.

Quick and easy.

Chapter 8

MOTHERS-IN-LAW

ALL OF MY CHILDREN WERE BORN BEFORE THEIR DUE DATES.
Unless you are a parent-to-be who is renovating an apartment that you really, really hope will be finished before the baby arrives, or you are waiting for grandparents to fly in from another country in time to be at the hospital, a baby coming before its due date is heaven. Pregnancy, at the end, is a bit hellish—and I say that as someone who had easy pregnancies. I was still downing a bottle of Tums a day just to be able to sleep without feeling like my esophagus was filled with fire ants.

Julia, my oldest, came eleven days early. Her birth was uneventful. I felt contractions in the morning while returning a mop to Bed Bath & Beyond in Chelsea. On the subway ride home, around 11 a.m., my lower abdomen began cramping, like my entire torso was the Liberty Bell (which—I've seen it—isn't much bigger than I was at the time), and someone was gonging it ever so slightly. Gooonngg. At 3 p.m. I called Michael and told him not to dilly-dally coming home from work. I was going to make meat loaf for dinner, but instead I ordered a pepperoni pizza and began washing clothes. Getting a load out of the dryer, talking to my sister on the phone, I had to stop chatting and hold on to the dryer door. GOOONNGG. "You need to go to the hospital," said my sister. I did, an hour or so later, and Julia was born in a very normal, moderately torturous fashion at 3:33 in the morning. I was also thirty-three years old. It's the only reason I can remember any of those details.

Once Julia was born, the nurse turned to Michael and said, "You better get going down to the lobby." We knew this was coming. During our tour of the labor and delivery ward a few weeks earlier, the guide explained that at Mount Sinai, where I birthed all three of my children, private rooms for new mothers aren't a thing. Unless you paid extra, you'd have a roommate. Everyone on the tour nodded blithely, because we were all New Yorkers. We understood that square feet didn't grow on trees, and if you wanted a private bathroom and a pullout couch, you should be giving birth in Missouri. The rules for getting a private room at Mount Sinai were:

1. The baby had to be outside the womb. No advance reservations.
2. There was a very limited number of private rooms, so the hospital recommended that a partner make haste to the lobby office as soon as the baby was born.
3. Different rooms were different prices, depending on the size and the view. As the hospital staff explained this to us, I imagined a salesperson pulling out a laminated card listing the rooms like time-shares. "This one is lovely. It's a corner unit, near the communal kitchen, and everyone wants to be

closer to that ice machine, right?" Prices ranged from $650 to $850. A night.

4. Partners who fainted at the sight of the bill would be escorted directly to a shared room.

5. Pay up front. Credit cards only.

Michael secured a room for me that wasn't the cheapest but also not the most expensive. The best feature was the view, which included Central Park and, if you squinted, our apartment building. My favorite thing about giving birth at Mount Sinai is that I can walk to my appointments—and birth, if absolutely necessary during a snowstorm or taxi strike—and see home from my bed.

James was born around noon (I think?) a couple of years later. Despite the fact that he was almost ten pounds, he was the easiest birth of my three kids. He came early because he was enormous, and my doctor thought that letting him continue to gestate until his due date would result in a dangerous delivery. I told her that my father was over eleven pounds when he was born, and I was a healthy nine and a half. Big babies are in our genes, I said. I am tall and strong and usually in a combative mood. I could handle a huge child. She was unmoved. "If he doesn't come by Friday, I'm scheduling you to be induced."

The good thing about being induced is that you can tick off all the preparations without being rushed. Mount Sinai has mothers check in at midnight on the day they'll be induced. The nurses start Pitocin, the drug that gets labor going, with the idea that by 7 a.m. when your doctor starts her shift, you are ready to have a baby. On the Sunday before I left for the hospital, I went to church, then got a pedicure with my dad, since my parents were already in town and my dad had developed those shell-like, old-man toenails that benefit from an industrial sawing off by a nail technician every now and then. After we finished our pedicures, I spent a while packing my hospital bag. That night, when Michael and I arrived at Mount Sinai, a midwife on staff at the hospital met me. She was probably in her late fifties, with wild, curly gray hair and a soft voice. She placed her hands around my belly firmly, like she was taking the baby by the shoulders to tell him something very important. She closed her eyes, breathed in loudly through her nose, and then looked at me.

"They told you this is a big baby, right?"

"Yes, that's why I'm being induced. They think he's almost ten pounds," I said.

"Listen. I don't want you to be worried," she said to me, running her palm back and forth over my stomach. "This baby is no more than eight pounds. I can tell. It's going to be an easy, smooth delivery. I promise."

First of all, I was not worried. Second, that was a ballsy thing to say. So many things can go sideways during a birth. I appreciated her confidence, but I also started to wonder if she was someone's oddball aunt who had wandered in off Madison Avenue to rub pregnant bellies.

The midwife was right that it was an easy, smooth delivery. My doctor was right that James was just shy of ten pounds. I suppose the lesson is that babies are unpredictable, and many people can be right in complicated situations. I lucked out that the head of the anesthesiology department at the hospital happened to be wandering the halls soon after I was admitted and asked if I'd like him to go ahead and put in my epidural, even though I wasn't yet having any contractions. I'm a woman who would ask for an epidural in the cab on the way to the hospital, so I immediately accepted his offer. To me, this was like ordering the chocolate soufflé for dessert at the same time you order your appetizers; it makes practical sense, and you get a seamless transition to bliss. When the first twinge of discomfort pinged my uterus a few hours later, while Michael and I were watching *Date Night* with Tina Fey and Steve Carell, I pressed a button, and that glorious numbing agent rushed right into my spine like holy water. James came out with approximately three pushes, surrounded by a dozen nursing students whom I'd given permission to run in and watch, after my labor and delivery nurse said she'd never witnessed a baby this big being born this easily. She held him up next to the scale like he was a prized catfish and told Michael to take a picture.

I had said a few days before that I didn't need a private room, this being my second child and all. But then I got high on my own power, and the nursing students were actually high-fiving me, and so I changed my mind. I turned to tell Michael that maybe he could, actually, see if any private rooms were available, but he was already heading toward the door. "Done! You earned it!" he yelled from the hallway.

The point of this chapter, however, is to talk about Sam's birth, and how it became one of my favorite stories to tell that involved my mother-in-law. He wasn't measuring as big as James did, so my doctor was content to let me go to my due date. We discussed an induction, just as an option, in case I was fed up. Of course, I never made it that far. My water broke eight days early while I was eating a chocolate cupcake at Magnolia Bakery on Columbus Avenue. Julia and James were across the street at their piano teacher's apartment. If you have children, you've probably heard the rule about how, once your water breaks, you need to deliver the baby within a certain window because bacteria can enter the amniotic sac (again??) once it's breached. That time frame might be two hours, it might be twenty-four; I never paid attention, which is soon going to be apparent. I picked up the kids from piano, went home, cooked lemon chicken for dinner, and decided that I would call my doctor and figure out what to do once Julia and James were asleep, around 7:30 or 8 p.m. I wasn't having any contractions, just soaking through Kotex with increasingly alarming speed. The less chaos in getting out the door the better, I reasoned. We would get the kids to bed, then call Michael's mother to come over. She would stay at our apartment, and the kids would get a full night's sleep and wake up to the happy news.

While Michael tucked in the kids in the back bedroom, I called my doctor, who was not pleased with me.

"Your water broke when?" she asked. I told her. "Ugh, Elizabeth. Please go to the hospital. I'm on call tonight. I will see you in an hour."

The induction date my doctor and I had tentatively put on the calendar was numerically in harmony with my older children's birthdays, all stairstepped, even, and single digits. My delay in wanting to go to the hospital might have been because I was sad Sam wouldn't have that induction birthday. I have never paid attention to any sort of numerology or horoscopes. This had nothing to do with that. My disappointment at Sam not having this perfectly coordinated birthday came solely from the fear that I'd never remember his date otherwise. I was forty-one when Sam was born. I was already having a hard time remembering things. Between my sister's three kids and mine, only one, other than Sam, has a double-digit, late-in-the-month birthday, and I have to look it up on my calendar every single year. That particular nephew is sixteen.

Once the kids were asleep, I finished packing a bag and told Michael to call his mother. My in-laws live just across Central Park on the Upper East Side, and a cab ride from their apartment to ours takes less than ten minutes, especially at night. Michael dialed his parents' number and went into the kitchen. I heard him talking in a low, excited voice, and then his tone changed just slightly, a dip downward. He said a few more words, hung up, and walked into the living room.

"So she's coming?" I asked, putting toiletries into my tote.

"No. Not exactly," he said.

"What do you mean?"

"She wants us to bring the kids to her house."

"And you told her no."

"I did not."

"You did not?"

"I did not."

"I'm confused. Your mother wants us to wake up our children and bring them to her apartment? On our way to the hospital? To deliver our baby? Who's probably running low on amniotic fluid by now?"

"That's correct."

"So, you are going to call your sister, then? Surely you did not tell your mother that we'd actually bring the kids to her."

"That is in fact what I told my mother, yes."

I have dozens of stories like this about my mother-in-law. If you've hung out with me at a cocktail party or worked with me since the year 2005, you've probably heard one or two. Maybe the one about her boiling brussels sprouts—she ate them for cancer prevention—in the hospitality suite at the hotel where our wedding guests stayed, so that the entire floor smelled like a sewage-treatment plant all weekend. She frequently finished hanging ornaments on the Christmas tree around noon on Christmas Day.

IT WAS AN UGLY COUCH ANYWAY

One Christmas morning, shortly after Michael and I got married, I came downstairs to a cold, dark kitchen, my mother-in-law in the middle of it asking if I'd like anything from Starbucks because she was about to make a run. Maybe a latte? A bagel? My children have come home from outings with her with wild stories. Nan was pulled over by a policeman on the West Side Highway and got a ticket! She couldn't find James's booster seat, so he was sitting on a stack of throw pillows she had in the trunk! When the kids were toddlers, if I asked her to bathe one of them while he was at her house, that child would inevitably arrive home not in the clothes I sent but with one of her trouser socks on each chubby leg and a scarf wrapped around his torso. "Oh, did you send clothes?" she'd say, waving a dismissive hand. "But look at what we found! He's so warm and cozy." My mother-in-law is quirky.

She is not at all what I imagined I'd get in a mother-in-law. In my previous dating experiences—which, admittedly, were few—my boyfriends' parents found me delightful. I had nice manners. I could make conversation. I liked sports and the theater and ate everything except salmon. I wrote thank-you notes and bought gifts and talked and smiled and talked and smiled and talked. Southern parents were always charmed. But I didn't fall in love with a Southerner. I fell in love with a man whose parents grew up in Inwood, on the northernmost tip of Manhattan, as children of Irish and Italian immigrants. They are New Yorkers through and through. Catholic. My mother-in-law thought George W. Bush should be prosecuted for war crimes. And then in walks a future daughter-in-law, an evangelical Christian from the South, who voted for the war criminal. (Once. I voted for Kerry in 2004.) When we got engaged—after Michael's first year of law school—he didn't call and tell his parents until a full day later, more than twenty-four hours, because he knew, deep down, they thought it was too soon. (It was not too soon. We dated for four years.) What I wanted was a future mother-in-law to pull me into a bear hug and say, "Oh, we have always *wanted* him to find a woman just like you!" What I got was a cool, "Welcome to the family," accompanied by an antique brooch she bought for me at an auction house. I'm not what she imagined, either.

Despite what you might conclude from the story surrounding Sam's birth, my mother-in-law is not self-centered. She doesn't expect the world to revolve around her in the least. Quite the opposite, actually. She lives to serve her family, to a point that becomes annoying at times. Could she pick up a pint of ice cream on her way over for dinner? She *could*, and she could also offer to drive to Ardsley, New York, an hour away, to that bakery that sells the cookies she sometimes gets for Christmas that she knows James really loves, if I want. It's really no trouble, she'll just leave for dinner a bit early and go to Ardsley on her way, it's hardly out of the way, it's fine, would I like her to do that? She does not take no for an answer easily. No soccer match or airport drop-off got by her—only you might get the following instructions: "I'm still taking you to LaGuardia, but I need you to meet me on the southwest corner of Ninth Avenue and Forty-Fourth Street. I'm meeting my upholsterer halfway through the Lincoln Tunnel to drop off a loveseat." (I'm exaggerating, but only the tiniest bit.) If one of my children expressed interest in a French horn she saw on a television commercial, my mother-in-law would say, "Oh, well, do you want to go to the Philharmonic? How about next Thursday?" Generosity is a strange thing to resent, but it can be exhausting when it comes without boundaries.

I've told the story of Sam's birth a hundred times, but I never mention the reason my mother-in-law didn't come over. My father-in-law was sick that day, and he did not want my mother-in-law to leave. He was nervous about being alone overnight. At the time, and for months and months afterward, I dismissed that part of the story, and I was still righteously indignant. But now, with a few years of hindsight, I feel differently. A dear friend's mother and I had lunch together about six months after I got married. This mother of my friend was named Susie. I was complaining about my mother-in-law, about a habit of hers I found strange or a way I felt left out or slighted. Susie looked at me with benign pity and said, "You have to remember that she has lived an entire life before she became your mother-in-law." She had lived through a marriage that wasn't always easy, because no marriages are, and she had raised children, which shatters you in a million ways. Be compassionate and gentle with her, Susie told me. I did not listen. But I get it now. My in-laws have been married for almost sixty years. Something about their dynamic demanded that my mother-in-law stay with her husband instead of sleeping at my apartment, which I'm sure she would have preferred. I made light of it, because it is a great story and I will do almost anything for a laugh. But the older I get, the more I see my mother-in-law with empathy instead of eye-rolling. It's a shame it took so long, because she is more frail and no longer able to do so many things with my kids that she used to. I wasted too many hours being annoyed instead of grateful.

The story of my mother and father getting engaged feels eerily similar to mine. They dated for a long time—six years. My mother was a Methodist from a small town. She had never met a Jewish person until she met my father. He was an only child (see: eleven-pound baby), spoiled and adored his entire life. I'm sure my grandparents weren't expecting him to fall madly in love with a *shiksa* from Mississippi. Shortly after my father proposed, the two of them went to dinner with my Jewish grandparents. My grandmother, Jennie, said something along the lines of, "Welcome to the family," and gave my mother a gold watch.

Michael was also sort of an only child. He was the only boy, and his two older sisters were in middle school when he was born. He was adored beyond measure. I was the interloper. The main difference in our engagement stories with our in-laws is that my mom still has her gold watch, and I can't for the life of me remember where I put that brooch.

When the subject of mothers-in-law comes up in a churchy crowd, people mention Naomi and Ruth from the Old Testament. I know there are other in-laws in the Bible, but Naomi and Ruth have the market cornered. Their story is that Naomi, an Israelite, moves with her husband and two sons to Moab where the culture and the gods were different, because there was a famine in Israel. Naomi's sons marry Moabite women—one named Orpah, which will only ever look like Oprah to any present-day reader of the Bible, and one named Ruth. All of the men die of unknown reasons, and Naomi is left with her daughters-in-law. The famine in Israel ends, and Naomi wants to return home, but she tells Ruth and Orpah to stay in Moab. Find new husbands, she tells them. Live your life. After some urging, Orpah decides to stay in Moab, but Ruth "clung" to Naomi. She says, "Your people will be my people and your God my God" (Ruth 1:16). Ruth chooses a country and a faith that is foreign to her, even as her mother-in-law practically demands that she not.

The story of Naomi and Ruth always made me uncomfortable,

because I would never, in a million years, have made the choice that Ruth made. Especially not after experiencing marriage and in-laws. I was Orpah, back with her old customs, everything familiar. As a young, married woman, I wanted my mother-in-law to bend to my expectations, cheer and celebrate what I was bringing to the table, not the other way around. I thought I was superior. Her people be my people? Her God my God? Her Starbucks my Starbucks? No way. Faithful, dedicated Ruth, meanwhile, became the mother of Obed, who was the father of Jesse, who was the father of King David. Orpah is lost to history. Ruth's name is written in the lineage of Jesus.

I don't think Ruth followed her mother-in-law because Naomi was a bag of fun. Naomi was *super depressed*. Ruth followed because God was calling her—to a new land, a new husband (surprise!), and to him. That's the only hope for mothers- and daughters-in-law, I believe. God has to be in the middle of it. We're doomed otherwise. God's gentle, persistent tugging at me to see my mother-in-law as a fellow suffering human—and a treasured child of his—instead of the constant impediment to my wishes has changed my heart. I still have a ways to go, but most of the time these days, I can look at her with grace and acceptance. I don't want her to be different. I can appreciate how playful she is with my children and how diligently she serves her family. When I see cracks or brittleness, where I used to complain or gloat, I now feel love. That's not my doing. That's a poultice of time and mercy. I am able to grieve what I wanted but didn't get and, well, move on.

———

We did wake up Julia and James and take them to my in-laws' apartment the night Sam was born. I was pissed about it. Instead of hopping in a cab by ourselves, we roused sleeping kids, packed backpacks for school the next day, explained that I was in labor, and dealt with the fallout from that news. Julia was elated. James was terrified. Because James was scared of me going to the hospital, Michael thought it was best to get the kids settled at his parents' while I checked in at Mount Sinai. They dropped me off in a cab and kept going the few blocks to my in-laws' apartment (admittedly, they did live very close to the hospital). It all turned out fine. Michael made it back as they were moving me to a delivery room. Sam was born quietly at a time that I cannot remember to save my life. My in-laws walked Julia and James over in the morning to see their new brother, and it was as sweet a reunion as I could have hoped for.

In the last few years of my grandmother Jennie's life, long after my grandfather died, my mother was the one who took care of her. I'm sure she felt the push-pull of relief and resentment that it was her in-laws who lived in town, while her own parents were out of state. I feel that every day. My mother modeled an uncomplicated selflessness, though. When my grandmother still lived in an apartment but needed someone to be with her at night, my mother would switch off nights with my grandmother's nurse, sleeping in the guest room at the apartment, bringing her the whitefish with the heads still on that she liked to eat, cleaning up accidents. I'd go with my mom some nights, because my grandmother's place was around the corner from my school. We would wake up in the morning, get a doughnut at Seessel's grocery store on the corner, and my mother would drive me to school before going back to my grandmother's to get her up and dressed. Eventually, my grandmother moved in with us. My mother treated her with such respect and tenderness every single day. It was a beautiful picture of sacrificial love. My grandmother died in our house when I was a sophomore in high school. My mother never got the adoration she deserved. I wonder if it was enough for her to remember that this woman raised the man she loved. It's so obvious, and yet we forget. We can't have one without the other.

ADVICE ON DEALING
WITH IN-LAWS

For: The Newly Engaged or Married

From: Me, Who Has Questionable Credibility

1. From the beginning, as much as possible, let your husband deal with his parents. Everyone tends to their own gardens, so to speak. If a difficult conversation needs to be had, let him have it with them. If someone needs to call about birthday reservations or picking up the grandkids, let it be him. You have your own parents.

2. There are going to be a dozen things surrounding your wedding that you want your in-laws to do differently. With most of them, no one will notice. My father-in-law demanded that we have a Catholic priest at our Episcopalian wedding, and he found one, and we had to make a special trip to Memphis to meet with the guy, and I was so annoyed. Then the priest dismissed me from the room—because, I'm guessing, I was baptized in a dunk tank at a nondenominational church—so that he could talk to Michael, the good Catholic. *Then* he made Michael sign a paper that declared he'd do everything in his power to raise our children Catholic. Guess what? We are married, my father-in-law was so happy to have that priest at the altar, our children were baptized in the Presbyterian church, and no one was struck by lightning. Pick your battles.

3. Within reason, let your mother-in-law do what she wants with your kids. My children have seen Broadway plays that were way, way over their heads and mildly inappropriate, because my mother-in-law loves Broadway and wants to share it with her grandchildren. Great! She took my daughter to *The Nutcracker* at Lincoln Center before she was two years old and spent half the time in the bathroom playing with the hand blower. Fine! Her money! Let your mother-in-law feed them whatever she wants. Waffle cones are not the hill you want to die on.

4. You cannot control what any grandparent gives your children for holidays and birthdays. I'm sorry. You *can* say, "Get her the rocking horse, but can it please stay at your house?" It helps if you live in a small apartment. You can also donate things and never tell your mother-in-law, which is much easier than trying to convince her to give your children "experiences." Don't even get me started.

5. You can try to split holidays fifty-fifty: one year, you spend Christmas with your family; the next year, with your in-laws. It may work for a time. Eventually, though, the system falls apart. Know this. As my friend Catherine Newman, the author and longtime Modern Manners columnist for *Real Simple*, once said—I'm paraphrasing—some years you have to spend it with whoever needs you more, even if it's not equal. Be flexible and compassionate when you don't get your way.

6. Be your best self to your in-laws' friends. Even if your charisma doesn't work on your mother-in-law, it might on her bridge partner. Behold, that friend praises you to your mother-in-law. Every bit helps.

7. Don't drive a wedge between your husband and his mother, even if it's small, like making fun of her to him. I have done this. I suffered the most. (Addendum: You should also be careful about complaining to your own mother about your mother-in-law. This can backfire.)

8. You don't have to go to every family gathering. Every once in a while, your husband can spend time with his parents without you. They only want to see him and the grandkids anyway.

9. If your mother-in-law greets you in a dark kitchen on Christmas morning and asks what you want from Starbucks, take a deep breath and order a chai latte and a morning bun.

Chapter 9

LOST IN TIMES SQUARE

WHEN MY SISTER WAS YOUNG—YOUNG ENOUGH THAT I, ALMOST four years younger, was not yet sent out into our neighborhood to tag along without a parent—she left our house in our quiet neighborhood in a suburb of Memphis to meet up with friends. "Mom! I'm going to Caydie's!" she said to my mother, who was probably in the front yard weeding with a tumbler of iced coffee sitting next to her. Long before iced coffee became a drink you could order at Starbucks or any old diner, my mother was taking her leftover mug of morning coffee, pouring it into a tall, turquoise plastic cup, and filling it with the ice cubes from our freezer that always looked to me like Saturn: round with irregular, chipped rings, like discs, around the middle where the ice maker mold punched them loose. Sometimes she added a Sweet'N Low. It was the only drink I remember her carrying outside to weed the vinca beds.

My mother, we learned later that day, heard, "I'm going to Amy's"—a different friend entirely.

When children get separated from their parents, it is almost always a result of a simple misunderstanding or insignificant choice. You thought we were meeting at the bottom of the waterslide; I thought we said the snack bar. Even the rare instances where something horrible happens, it's because a parent turned to talk to a neighbor for a few minutes too long or left a window open that they normally lock. That's why the fear of losing your child or not stopping them before they step into traffic is so terrifyingly tangible. Because it doesn't take much. You don't have to be a neglectful parent, just one who heard a long *a* sound and assumed "Amy" instead of "Caydie."

Of course, my sister was not lost. She was at Caydie's. But later in the afternoon, when my mother needed her to come home, she knocked on Amy's door, only to be told that Holland had definitely not been there all day. Assuming she'd been abducted on her bike on the way there, my mother called the police. Holland came home an hour or so later to find officers and flashing lights up and down our street and had to explain to all of the hysterical adults that the only tragedy of the day was that apparently our mother was losing her hearing.

I once lost my dad in a hardware store when I was four or five years old. It was the classic scenario where the kid is mesmerized by a display wall of plumbing fixtures, then comes out of her trance to realize her dad is nowhere in sight. For me, the panic did not set in immediately. I started walking up and down a couple of aisles, and just as my stomach started to churn, I saw my dad. I ran to him and threw my arms around his legs, only to look up and see a face looking down at me that definitely did not belong to my father. I can't remember if the man was kind or amused; I was so embarrassed to be hugging the pants leg of a stranger. Thankfully, my dad rounded the corner a second later, gave me a wry smile, and looked at me like I'd played a very good joke. He said something along the lines of, "There you are. I assume you found the socket wrenches you were looking for?"

I handle losing my kids in a similar way to my dad. If there's panic, it's mild, and I don't show it. The worst that can happen, I always think, is that I eventually have to ask an employee at the grocery store/clothing store/amusement park to page my kid over a loudspeaker or weather the judgmental looks of other parents, which I can handle. A couple of years ago, as we picnicked in Central Park with friends and got caught up in conversation, we stopped paying attention to my youngest child, who was two at the time. After a while, I heard a man shouting, "Whose child is this?" and before I could say, "Um, mine?" the man and his wife, both with *very concerned* faces, began marching Sam back to us.

"Just so you know, he was playing with a dead mouse on the hill over there," the man said.

"Oh, I did not know. Thank you so much for telling me," I said.

"I found a mouse," said Sam.

"I know, baby. But next time, just look."

The couple stood and watched in horror as I sanitized Sam's palms and handed him a piece of pizza. If New York has taught me anything, it's that the dead mouse is probably not the dirtiest thing my toddler will touch in a day.

New York has also taught me that my kids are incredibly safe, even if they are lost. I know what you're thinking. It's the Big City, and it's dangerous, and crime is up, at least at the time of this writing (or always and forever without end, if you are speaking to my mom). You are right. It is a big city. And the world can be dangerous. And crime is up, although it is everywhere, and it is still lower than it was when I moved to New York City, and it's always been lower than it is in my hometown, ahem. But New York has a lot going for it. Think about how much more likely kids are to be hurt in a car accident versus a violent crime. You know which teenagers aren't driving? New York City teenagers. I think about times in my life I have been most frightened and vulnerable, and without fail, they were when I was alone or isolated. I have a horrendous sense of direction, so as a new driver I got lost dozens of times driving home at night and ended up in an unfamiliar neighborhood where I had to stop at a gas station and ask for directions. As a kid I took wrong turns on my bike and ended up alone on an empty street with no one around to help. Apologies to all of the nice families I babysat for as a junior high schooler, but I was terrified after dark in your giant homes in deathly quiet neighborhoods, where I had to lock fifteen different doors that led to the outside. When my now-thirteen-year-old began babysitting her brothers, there were three families on our floor and a twenty-four-hour doorman downstairs who knew to block the exit with his full body if Sam came careening through the lobby on his scooter before we could catch him. We have always felt remarkably safe.

Still, like most parents, I feel safer once my kids can memorize my phone number. I wonder sometimes if Gen X parents are especially neurotic about their kids knowing their cell phone number because we came of age without them. We are the generation that graduated from college with no cell phones and grew into adulthood, marriage, and parenthood as technology matured on a parallel path: chunky, hot-dog-sized Nokias to flip phones to smartphones, all in the same decade. Cell phones still hold some magical sway over us, because we remember what it was like to make plans over email (also still in its infancy) and have to stick to them as if we'd signed a blood pact.

So we make our kids repeat our cell phone numbers back to us over and over, shortly after they learn to talk, and we say things like, "If you get lost, find a *mom*. A MOM, do you hear me? A mom will help you. If you have to find a dad, find one with kids. That's how you know he's a dad, okay? Actually, nevermind. Just find a mom." In September 2018 Michael and I took Julia and James, ages eight and six at the time, to a Paul Simon concert at Madison Square Garden. Our hesitation at buying expensive concert tickets for young kids was outweighed by our fear that Paul Simon would die before they had another chance to hear him live.[1] As we entered the arena, the crowd began to press together, narrowing up a flight of stairs. I became distracted by an actor I couldn't place, standing in front of me with his two daughters—it was Dan Futterman, who played Val, Calista Flockhart's fiancé, in *The Birdcage*—and lost sight of James for a few seconds. He'd been herded along with the mass of people, all of whom were two feet taller than he was. A minute later we caught up to him, and I realized that, at six years old, he still did not know either my or Michael's phone number. Immediately I took a pen out of my purse and wrote it on his forearm. "We'll work on memorizing it later," I said to him, before settling into our seats. And we did. And it's come in very, very handy. Except the one time I lost James in Times Square on Christmas Eve.

---

1.   Michael and I ran into Paul Simon and his wife, Edie Brickell, on our honeymoon in Tulum, Mexico, in 2005. We were touring the Mayan ruins on the hottest day I can remember, and I noticed Edie Brickell first, because I loved her, but quickly became alarmed about the pale, sweating, shuffling old man next to her who looked like he was seconds away from stroking out. It was Paul Simon. He was wearing a Mets hat. I've worried about him once a week ever since.

I'm going to tell you this story now, and you're going to think I'm a bad parent. Or at least a casually inattentive one. You'd be right. I get distracted easily. I read books on the playground instead of watching Sam. I have a lot of faith in the majority of New Yorkers not being criminals, but mostly, I have a lot of faith in my kids' common sense. And just to be clear, in the context of this story—which turns out well, don't worry—James is not even my kid with the most highly tuned street smarts. Not by a long shot.

A couple of months after I wrote my cell phone number on James's arm at the concert, on Christmas Eve 2018, Michael took Julia and James ice-skating. It was one of the first Christmases in a few years that our family was staying in New York instead of traveling to Memphis, where my mom lives, or to my sister's house in Charleston, South Carolina. Instead of packing last-minute presents and heading to the airport, we were enjoying a slow, lazy Christmas Eve with no plans. Bryant Park has an ice-skating rink that opens during the winter, and at the holidays it's surrounded with glass-sided kiosks selling jewelry and hand-knitted hats, as well as some larger huts pumping out food and hot chocolate. If you get there right when it opens it's pretty empty, and it's the only ice rink in Manhattan that is free if you bring your own skates. Our nephew, Luke, who was in high school, met Michael and the kids and skated with them most of the morning, while I stayed home with baby Sam. Around 11 a.m. Michael texted me. He thought I could come down when Sam woke up from his morning nap and meet them for lunch, then maybe we could trade places. He'd take Sam home, and I'd hang out with Luke and the big kids until they were ready to leave. I said yes and hopped on the subway.

We ate some very expensive ramen, Michael left, and around 2 p.m. everyone had had their fill of ice-skating. Luke mentioned that he wanted to get one last thing for his mom, Michael's sister, Lynn, for Christmas: a photo of the two of them at a Mets game, printed and framed. I knew there was a Walgreens a few blocks away, so we sent the photo to be printed through the app and started walking from the edge of Bryant Park, on Forty-Second Street and Sixth Avenue, to the Walgreens on Forty-Second Street and Broadway, smack-dab in the middle of Times Square. The sidewalks were wide and calm as we crossed Sixth Avenue, but as we got closer to Broadway, foot traffic picked up. Christmas Eve is busy in Times Square. Tourists are in town, Broadway shows are happening, and there is more than one Lids store, it feels like, in a five-block radius. The Times Square Walgreens is, like many big stores that take up a lot of acreage in suburban areas (Target, Home Depot, Models), a stacked affair in New York. Stores have to go up and down, not spread out side to side. We entered a revolving door into a modest-sized storefront and realized our luck: the photo department was on the ground floor. Luke and I went up to the counter to retrieve his printed photo, while Julia wandered over to the frames to start looking.

In tense situations you can never tell how much time has passed. Retelling them gets tricky for that exact reason. Give it too little time, and the story loses the drama. Too much, and no one is having fun anymore. I'm going to say five minutes passed before Luke—yes, Luke, not me, the mother—said, "Where's James?" And I responded with the classic juvenile phrase of blame shifting: "I thought he was with you." A quick scan down the few aisles on the ground floor revealed that he was definitely not there.

"I'll go up," Luke said, and sprinted toward the escalator that led to the second, larger floor.

A prime lesson I've learned as a parent is that when you think you may have become separated from a child, head to the danger zone first. Don't waste time searching the beach. Your kid isn't going to drown in sand. Go directly to the water. Don't bother looking through the frozen food section before you make sure the front door hasn't been breached. So I immediately went back through the revolving door onto the corner of Forty-Second Street and Broadway.

Things would have been much less stressful if Julia had been the one to get lost. Of course, Julia wouldn't have gotten lost, because she is my hunting dog, the pointer, the one always a step ahead of where I need to go, whining and urging me in the direction she thinks is best. She has an innate sense of direction, like her father. James, on the other hand, is like me. When we walk through the city, our minds are usually elsewhere. I talk to myself. I miss my turn. I go blocks out of the way and circle back. Who knows what is happening in James's brain, but I suspect it is something similar. He's daydreaming about a type of bird he once saw on vacation or trying to remember what an artichoke is called. New York City streets, with their crosswalks and tourists and bike lanes with speeding delivery men, require focus that doesn't come naturally to either James or me. If I'm so much as listening to a podcast or even wearing a hat—don't ask, it makes me feel like my vision is stunted—while walking, I will forget where I'm going and pass it right by. It shouldn't have surprised me in the least that James did not notice us walk through the Walgreens revolving door.

When I got outside it was dark, not because it was late, but because there was scaffolding covering the block. I scanned the sidewalk, but it was dense with people. Everything was shadowy. *Maybe he's just right here*, I thought. *Maybe I don't need to scream his name like a lunatic and draw attention.* But as a few more seconds passed, I realized that every second I didn't locate him, he could be getting farther away. The block was chaotic. Groups of tourists pushed past me, their bodies creating slow-moving barriers that obstructed my view in every direction, blocking any chance of seeing a four-feet-tall human in the distance. Trying to spot him while walking down the block, not knowing for sure which direction he'd gone, felt to me like those reality show games where contestants are biting through king cakes at Mardi Gras. They're trying to luck out and locate the plastic baby, only one contestant always gets too frantic, and the baby falls on the floor while they're chomping, chomping, chomping, and they waste so much time eating cake looking for the baby *that's right there at their feet.* At the intersection of Broadway and Seventh Avenue, cars were honking and pushing up against throngs of people struggling to cross before the light changed. *Please don't let him have crossed that intersection*, I pleaded. I imagined going home and telling Michael that I'd lost our son. And then I saw it. A braided yarn tail on the top of a ski hat swinging in the distance. He was just at the end of the block.

"James! James!" I shouted over the traffic noise.

The grey and blue cap spun, and I could see his face. "Mom!" Suddenly, the roar of the city went quiet in my head, and all I could hear was his breathing and his cries as he ran back toward me. As he crashed into me, and I kissed the top of his head, saying, "I'm so sorry, I've got you, I've got you," he kept repeating something into my chest. I couldn't make it out at first. Then he lifted his head, his face red and wet, and said, "I asked a mom, and she said no!"

"What? What are you talking about?" I asked.

He repeated it. "I asked a mom, and she said no."

"Asked a mom what?"

"For her phone!"

"You mean you asked a mom to call me, and she said no?"

"YES!" He started crying again.

I walked James through the door of Walgreens to find Luke and Julia and let them know James was safe. We finished paying for Luke's photo, and I knelt down and asked James to tell me what happened, step by step.

"Well, I didn't see you walk through the door, and I kept walking down the street," he said. "And when I realized I wasn't with you, I remembered to stay where I was and not leave the block."

"Right. That's great. Stay where you are, don't go looking for us. That's exactly what you should have done. Good for you," I said.

"And then I stopped a mom," James said.

"Okay. And what did you say?"

"I said, 'Give me your phone, and take off the security code.'"

"Say that again?"

"I said, 'Give me your phone, and take off the security code.' And she said no and walked away."

Now, it is unlikely I'll ever know what went through that woman's mind. I can venture a few guesses. The simplest explanation for her refusal to help my lost child is that, considering it was Times Square during the holidays, she was a visitor from another country and may not have understood James's hysterical sobbing English on a cacophonous sidewalk. It is possible, though, that she assumed he was a tiny, bold thief who flustered unsuspecting tourists with the phrase, "Gimme your cell phone, and take off the security code," while his accomplice picked their back pockets. Had James led with, "I've lost my mom. Could you help me call her?" instead, I'm fairly certain he would have gotten a different response. Later, as we calmly dissected the events and what everyone did right and wrong, we discussed his approach. I told him how proud I was that he remembered to stay put on the block rather than wander farther away. I asked him to repeat my phone number, to make sure he knew it. (He did.) I asked him what he would have done if I hadn't found him quickly.

"I would have gone into a store and asked the cashier to call you. Or into a building with a doorman," he said.

"Exactly. Perfect," I answered.

Doormen will never cease to be multipurpose heroes and security blankets to me. In all my years in New York, I've met only one who I wouldn't trust to babysit my children, honest to God.

The weeks that followed our Times Square incident were a little shaky for James. Shortly after New Year's, Michael took him to Whole Foods. He told James he was walking to the next aisle to grab some pasta. Three minutes later Michael heard an announcement over the intercom. "Can Michael Passarella please come to customer service? Michael Passarella, you are needed at customer service." Waiting there was a slightly jumpy James, relieved that his relocation efforts had worked this time.

One afternoon, about a month later, at school pickup, I stopped to talk to a friend on my way toward the exit from the school auditorium. James followed another mother—who, in his defense, was pushing the same City Mini stroller I was—only to realize once outside that the woman was not his mother, and his mother was nowhere to be seen. Still in the auditorium, assuming James was playing on the stage with his friends, I ignored two phone calls from an unknown number—James calling me from another parent's cell phone. I know, I know. It was fine. He walked around to the front entrance of the school and took a seat with Candy, the security guard, until I listened to my messages and found him about fifteen minutes later.

He's slower on the trigger these days.[2]

I tell the story of losing James in Times Square all the time. To me, it is encouraging. Teach children what to do in an unlikely event. Experience unlikely event. Witness children remember (almost all of) what you taught them. Rejoice at unlikely event ending on a happy note. Feel proud of parenting. And I do. There is no doubt in my mind that James feels more confident on his own, having had that experience and come out okay.

But it also gives me immense hope for the lost. For myself, who is often, in the temporal and cosmic sense, very lost. It gives me hope, because we usually botch the message, just like James. I'd instructed my child on what to say to the mom with the phone, and he messed it up. It's completely understandable, given the fact that he was six and separated from his family in one of the busiest intersections in the country. Still, I might have found him sooner, or he might have felt less panicked, if he'd told the woman he had lost his mother, and could she please let him call her? Instead, he stayed stuck until I screamed his name.

I've thought about that since, how often I stay lost because I'm forgetting—or ignoring—the instructions. My overconfidence leads me to frequently follow 90 percent of the steps but assume I can wing it in the end. (I've never read the full instructions on how to tie-dye or egg dye, which is why neither ends well in my

---

2. In fact, earlier this year James neglected to board a subway train behind his dad and got left on the platform, while Michael banged on the windows of the subway car, trying to get his attention as the train pulled away. My mother has never heard this story, and she just had a heart attack. Maybe you did too. But can I pause for a moment and note that we all watch the plucky kid from *Sleepless in Seattle* fly across the country and find his way to the Empire State Building, and we think, *What a precocious little nugget*, yet we can't give the same benefit of the doubt to our own children in much lower-stakes situations? James was, once again, totally fine. Michael took the subway one stop, raced to the opposite side of the platform, and went back. The kid hadn't moved.

household.) I do this with God on a daily basis. Yes, I remember a vague reference to being slow to speak and quick to listen, sure, but I'm going to put my own spin on that, based on how I'm feeling toward my family members at this precise moment, thank you. I'm demanding a woman in Times Square give me her phone and take the security code off instead of admitting I've lost my way. And lo and behold, my situation does not improve. This is a pattern, me botching the message. And the worst part is that, unlike James, who nailed it on the next try, I will never get the words exactly right. I am destined to be asking a stranger to give me her phone and take off the security code forever.

The whole crux of the Christian faith is that we cannot save ourselves. This is meant to be good news, although for people like me, who pride ourselves on being supremely capable, it feels irritating at times. Even when I have a win—I succeed at being gentle with my child! I forgive someone who hurt me, despite the fact that I really didn't want to! I am humble for a few minutes in my day!—I know that I can't fix the brokenness inside me or overcome my own sin. For people who don't share my faith, this sounds totally depressing, I know. And entire self-help sections of bookstores tell you otherwise. I know this too. For some reason it is easier to believe that we can muscle our way to better, more fulfilled selves, rather than accept that we are hopelessly flawed and all of those efforts are going to be temporary. It doesn't mean we are idiots. Or weaklings. We know the phone number. We stay on the block when we are lost. We use the tools God gave us: brains and senses of humor. But ultimately, we cannot always find our way back when we are lost. He has to come get us.

In an episode of the *Mockingcast*, an excellent podcast from Mockingbird Ministries in Charlottesville, Virginia, the hosts—all

Episcopal priests—were discussing the movie *Tangled*. One host in particular thinks it is the best Disney movie ever made. I tend to agree. His point is that we spend most of the movie following Rapunzel and Flynn Rider and waiting for them to fall in love and wondering if Mother Gothel will catch them. But the most touching part of the movie is that the king and queen, Rapunzel's parents, are sending lanterns out into the sky once a year, remembering her, longing for her, looking for her. That is how God is with us. We are missing the revolving door to Walgreens and fumbling around in Times Square, but he is looking for us, always. He wants to pull us back so badly that he sent his Son to die for our sins, so that we can stop striving and simply accept that gift of salvation.

When I am lost, I don't have to remember the way home. I don't have to get the message right. Because he is out on the crowded sidewalk, looking for me.

Chapter 10

I USED TO BE A
DOG PERSON

ONE NIGHT LAST DECEMBER, WHILE OUR CHILDREN WERE AT *THE* *Nutcracker* with Michael's mother and sister, he and I met up to do some Christmas shopping. After about an hour of wandering through stores, we stopped at The Smith, a large, loud American bistro directly across the street from Lincoln Center. It was packed, with dozens of people waiting outside for their names to be called for a table. We squeezed through the crowd at the door and found a sliver of counter space at the bar, directly behind a man and his drinking companion, which happened to be a black, shaggy-haired dog, sitting politely on a barstool. It was a very good-looking and well-behaved one, but still a dog, wagging its tongue inches away from a neat pile of martini olives.

I'm not sure what the rules are for dogs in restaurants. I know that New York City has some quirky exceptions, and people take their dogs into stores and on subways. But I was once in an airport during March Madness, and North Carolina happened to be playing during my layover. I found a sports-themed restaurant with the game on and tried to sit down at the bar, which was the only seat close enough to see the TV. Julia was with me. She was four at the time. As I asked the bartender for a beer, he shouted at me that we'd have to move immediately. My kid couldn't sit at the bar, he said, because she was underage. Fair. But while leaning over the dog's head to signal the bartender that December night, I thought, *Surely the same must apply to a Schnauzer.*

Michael and I drank our Manhattans standing up, while the dog sat contentedly next to us. It did not appear to be any type of support animal—other than emotional, I guess, as that category is vague and hard to police. (I'd question whether the guy really needed his emotional support animal when he was already at a bar, which in my mind serves the same purpose.) Maybe the man owned the restaurant, and the dog was considered family. No one seemed to be bothered by its presence except the two of us, who really wanted a seat. I looked at the dog—this quiet, sweet-faced dog—and felt only hostility. I hated the dog. And the dog's owner, for assuming his dog deserved a prime seat at a crowded bar at a popular restaurant at one of the busiest times of the year in New York. That is when I realized I'd fully crossed over to being a non-dog person. It took about thirty years. But here we are.

———

I was the kid who found an abandoned baby squirrel in the backyard and carried it around in the front pocket of her T-shirt, feeding it milk with an eyedropper, until the local nature center agreed to take it. I made my mother pull over to coax a stray dog stranded in the median of the highway into our car. In a majority of photos from my early life, I am holding something feathered or furry—a neighbor's kitten, a duckling from a friend's farm, a turtle, a rabbit, a giant parrot. I begged for a pet from the moment I could talk.

When I was four, we got two cats. My sister, who was almost eight, and I entered the home of a family friend who had a litter of cats with the instruction that we could get *one*. But when we picked up one of the gray tabbies to nuzzle and coo at her, she held on to her sister, their sleepy little bodies stretching and stretching to stay attached to each other by their front paws. When we put one down and picked up the other, the same thing happened, like a seesaw. Holland and I cried to our mother: "Couldn't we please have both of them? Look! They can't be separated." And she relented. Maybe because there were two of us, two of them. Each girl got a cat. We named them Laverne and Shirley after our favorite television show.

A week after we brought Laverne and Shirley home, we took them to their first appointment at the vet. The vet said, "Laverne and Shirley are perfectly healthy, but you need to change their names. These kittens are male." We renamed them Blitz and Bully, after the two bulldog mascots of the football team at Mississippi State University, where my grandfather went. Originally, Blitz was my cat, and Bully was my sister's. But then Holland would demand that we switch, because I was being too rough with my cat, and she wanted to give him a break. I'd grab the cat's front legs as he was walking by the chair I was sitting in and pull him up over the arm into my lap. Once, in a fit of anger at my sister, I dangled Holland's cat—who knows which one it was at that moment—over the second-floor banister and threatened to drop him to see if he'd land on his feet.

I matured, eventually, and became gentler. And it didn't really matter whose was whose anyway, since no one could tell Blitz and Bully apart. They were identical; for a while we painted their claws with different nail polish colors. Then when I was nine, Bully darted across the driveway one afternoon as my mother was backing out in our station wagon. She ran over his tail, crushing it, but thankfully missing any vital organs. When I came home from school, my mother told me that Bully was at the vet. He'd be fine, she said, but he was having his tail amputated. (The sharpest memory I have from that day was learning the word *amputate*.) He returned the next morning with a shaved rear and barely a nub where his tail had been. I tried to coax him out from under the guest bed for days after his surgery. When he finally emerged, he walked on an angle, occasionally falling sideways for a few weeks. Without his tail he had to renegotiate his balance. But we could tell the two cats apart after that.

When I was ten I asked for and got a hamster. I named him Nibbles. We had Nibbles for a few months, and then one morning I heard a crash in the room where we kept his cage on a high table. I walked in to find the glass cage on the floor, sawdust shavings scattered everywhere, and Bully in the middle, his tongue scraping one side of his open mouth, then the other. Family lore is that he swallowed Nibbles whole. There wasn't a drop of hamster blood anywhere. It's possible that Nibbles escaped through a crack in the wall, but there weren't any cracks in the walls. And Bully looked guilty.

After the hamster debacle, I started begging for a dog. The hamster had been a mistake. No one liked playing with Nibbles, since all he did was run up and down the sleeves of your shirt, and we had to keep the cats out of the room whenever he was out of his cage. I knew I'd spent too much of my pet capital on him, though, and my next ask would need to be strategic. My father was not going to get a dog for nostalgic or practical reasons. He did not grow up with cocker spaniels, for example, and care about giving his children a love like he had with Bubbles or what have you. He did not hunt. There would be no bird dogs or retrievers for that purpose. My father did have excellent style, though—stick with me here—and appreciated well-designed clothes, jewelry, and kitchen gadgets. He prized cleverness—in kids, dogs, and anything else sentient that crossed his path. I just had to find a breed that was known to be smart and handsome, according to his standards.

With my mom, I only needed to act pitiful enough to wear her down. One weekend morning my mother and I were shopping in Germantown, the suburb of Memphis where we lived, and we saw a litter of puppies in the window of Saddles N' Such, an equestrian supply store. The puppies were Jack Russell terriers, and the location should have been a red flag. Jack Russells are a breed of dog that is devastatingly gorgeous and also evil. Please do not write to me to tell me stories of your gentle, angelic Jack Russell terrier. I'm not one to throw aspersions, but yours must have a little Basset Hound in him. Pure Jack Russells were bred to live on horse farms and hunt foxes in narrow holes. If you wrap both of your hands around one, it's like holding a high-powered DustBuster swathed in fur. Their bodies hum. And they are ferociously territorial. As puppies, though, they are divine: smooth, creamy white with rust, brown, and black markings on their faces. These dogs were like preppy little saddle shoes: dignified and the color of good scotch.

The shop owner couldn't stop talking about how intelligent they were. Sold. I picked one out, named him Kip on the spot, and asked my mom if we could talk to Dad and come back later. She said yes. But by the next day, the puppies were sold. I cried in my bed all night. "I just wanted *KIP*," I sobbed. I heard my mother in the next room tell my father to fix it. "She really wanted that dog," she said. My father admitted that they were beautiful animals. He started asking around to see if anyone in Memphis had a lead. A few months later, some friends of friends called. They had a litter for sale in Midtown Memphis. Did we want to come pick one out? I chose one of the smallest of the bunch, a full white puppy with chestnut markings on his face that looked like a mask. The owners had named him Batman. I changed it to Bandit. We took him home a couple of weeks later and slowly watched the innocence and cuteness drain from his body, replaced by raw psychosis.

Bandit was smart, but he was bad. He barked incessantly and would not follow commands. We took him to an obedience school that met in the parking garage of Clark Tower, a huge office building near our house. He did not sit or heel or stay. The obedience school told us they were sorry, but they could not give Bandit a passing certificate. He wanted to chase cars. If one was moving slowly enough, he'd snap at the tires, which did give us pause on how intelligent he really was. He once yanked the leash so violently to get at a passing truck that he broke my mother's thumb. We took him to Jack Russell races out in the country, where lots of Bandits would line up and chase a rabbit skin on a string through a hole in a hay bale, while their owners stood around hoping this would wear them out enough to get some peace and quiet at home that night.

I've known dogs that were wild and stupid, who chased squirrels and cars and got themselves stuck under fences. But most of them were lovable dummies who would also put their heads in your lap and let the baby fall asleep on their rumps. Not Bandit. He would settle in every night for an evening of mind games and torture. We were always on edge. Terriers tend to be possessive and snippy, but dealing with Bandit was like trying to get past a den of vipers. Once he'd chosen his beloved for the night—usually me or my mother—he would curl up nearby, often under the covers, and wait. If another person moved too close to the bed or couch, he'd start to rumble with rage. His lips would curl back, revealing all of his teeth, and he'd growl a long, low growl, then suck in a lungful of air with a snarling wheeze. My dad could manage to get into bed, if Bandit was nestled with my mom, only by snarling and growling back. I'm not joking. My father, a grown man, would act like a dog as he crawled into his own bed, until Bandit backed off and went to sleep. The cats took to sleeping on our pillows, far away from the dog, with one paw stretched protectively across our chests.

My family moved to a new house a couple of years after we got Bandit, and his behavior deteriorated to the point that even our extended family didn't like coming over and dealing with him. Our next-door neighbor had a dog named Cowboy that Bandit despised. If someone in the house so much as said the word *cowboy*, Bandit went nuts, speeding from window to window, howling and barking at top volume. "He has a wire loose," my dad would say. "Those dogs are supposed to live on horse farms," my mother said. I defended him, but it got harder. Blitz and Bully got older and took to even more extreme sleeping measures, curling up together on top of the dryer in the laundry room.

On the morning of my sixteenth birthday, I came downstairs dressed to go to the DMV for my driving test. I was wearing a blue, green, and yellow color-block turtleneck from the Gap. Bandit was asleep, his body coiled into a warm little cream puff on the back cushion of an armchair in the open living-kitchen area. Giddy about being hours away from having a driver's license, I skipped over to the dog, leaned my face into his, and cheerfully kissed his snout. Bandit was startled, and he snapped, sinking his teeth into the side of my upper lip. Instinctively, I pulled away, while Bandit hung on, tearing one side of my lip in half. Screaming, I ran to the kitchen sink, where my mother managed to wash away enough blood to see the damage. She took me to the hospital, where the doctor immediately called in a plastic surgeon. The surgeon pieced the jagged wound back together, while another doctor explained to my parents that, good news, he was not required to report a dog bite to animal control if the dog bit its owner. I qualified. Bandit was off scot-free. Meanwhile, I insisted on keeping my midday appointment at the DMV. I passed the driving test and walked over to the chair where they took your photo. The employee looked at me, swollen, stitched up, with a bandage covering much of my right cheek and chin. She asked if I wouldn't like to take the picture at a later date. They could issue me a temporary license, she said, and I could come back when my mouth had healed. "No, thank you. I am fine," I said stubbornly. I'd waited and worked hard, and I wanted that laminated plastic card with the photo in my hot little hand when I walked out of the building. So I smiled behind the bandage. Snap! She took the picture.

I still have the license. The photo is a little dark and blurry, making it hard to see the flesh-colored bandage. I am smiling with half of my mouth upturned; the other side is numb and flat, from the downward slant of my right eye all the way to my chin. Unless you know the backstory, you might glance at the photo and think that I had a neurological condition that left half of my face paralyzed. The fact that I now know people who have dealt with temporary palsy or permanent facial paralysis makes me feel bad that my friends and I laughed our immature, sixteen-year-old heads off at my license for years. But I'm glad it's still around as a reminder for two reasons. One, given a few years I think I would have taken the DMV employee's offer to come back later for a better photo. In college I doubt I would have sacrificed the chance to look pretty on my ID for a funny story or immediate gratification. In high school I did not care what that picture looked like, only what it represented. Good for me. Two, whenever I had a moment of weakness with that dog, I'd inevitably have a reason to pull out my driver's license, and the universe would remind me of his true nature.

A year later, on Christmas Eve, I reached down to drop a piece of leftover table food in Bandit's bowl while he was eating, and he bit a gash in my thumb. The summer after I graduated from high school, he launched at me from his post guarding my mother's ankles as I tried to lounge next to her in bed. His teeth punctured my left cheek in three places; the same plastic surgeon from four years before sewed me up again. After that, we put him down. The cats, who died in quick succession a couple of years before Bandit, were lovingly laid in old shoeboxes with their favorite cleaning rags from the laundry room and buried in the backyard of that house. Bandit got no such honor. I like to think his body was cremated by the vet and his ashes scattered in a foxhole, where he should have lived all along.

———

Ever since my father accidentally backed over me with the car when I was ten years old, I've had a hard time walking behind a parked car that's running. My gut tenses up. Sometimes I feel nauseated for a split second. The same sensation comes over me when a dog gets close to my face. I take in a sharp breath and clench every time, no matter how friendly or adorable or old or blind the poor pup is. (Actually, the blind ones are quite dangerous.) In the time it takes me to blink, I see that dog snapping at my face with bared teeth. My sister has had two golden retrievers in the past twenty years, both of them big, bumbling darlings who could sit with their faces inches from my toddler children waving a drumstick and not make a move. The minute one of my kids would lean down to kiss the dog's head or snout, I'd leap to intercept them as if they were about to touch a hot pan. When they ask if they can pet a dog in our building elevator, I say yes, but not near its mouth. I try to smile and be chill, but I've also become a person who hears strangers say, "Oh, she's wonderful with kids. She'd never bite," and responds, under my breath, "Until she does." I wish I could get back to the carefree dog lover I was as a kid, but I can't.

I suppose if I hadn't experienced the trauma of living with a pet that was daily trying to eat me alive, I might feel differently. Blitz and Bully were wonderful pets, dare I say dog-like in their affection and playfulness, and I still love cats. Michael is highly allergic, or else I'd get one. I like other people's dogs, for the most part. I am keenly aware of the comfort and companionship a good dog can provide, how they sense when you are sad, how on their best days they seem human. But I also live in an apartment, in a city where I would have to walk the dog every time he needed to poop or stretch his legs. Dogs are messy. Even if you buy one of the many crossbreeds that doesn't shed, he still has paws that get muddy and saliva that leaves snail-like trails on upholstery. I do not have a mudroom or even a place to put a dog bed that wouldn't be a sacrifice. When

I think about the way people describe dogs as guileless sidekicks who want nothing more than your attention and love, I think, *Yes, yes, okay, but I have children for that.* Even if I'd never had Bandit, even if I still harbored the same warmth toward dogs I did as a kid, I currently have no extra time or attention or affection to give. When my older two children bring up getting a dog, I remind them that I gave them a baby brother three years ago, and he's more fun. He can play Jenga.

My friends, however, are weak. Every friend of mine who gets a puppy inevitably confesses that it is harder than having a newborn. Just before school started in September this year, I took James on the train to Washington, DC, to spend the night with my old college roommate, Catherine, and celebrate her middle child's birthday. Their dog, Biscuit, a Labradoodle puppy purchased during the early days of the pandemic, was having her period. Catherine explained to me, with a tight smile and a tremor in her voice, that the vet had told them to wait to spay Biscuit until she'd completed her first menses. Catherine, like me, has three needy children, and so I watched with pity as my already exhausted friend spent the weekend walking around her house with a wet rag, wiping up tiny blood droplets from her expensive furniture as Biscuit swanned from chair to chair without a care in the world. She didn't *say* she wanted Biscuit to disappear in a mysterious dognapping—the kids would be devastated, obviously—but I sensed it.

In theory, I understand that kids plus dogs is some sort of picturesque ideal, but in reality it does not make sense to me. Parents of young children are already operating on thin margins. A puppy is too much work for people who are still potty training humans. The rules should be (1) dog must be in the home before you have children, (2) dog can be adopted during the years with young children, but said dog must be house-trained (i.e., not a puppy), or (3) dog can be brought into the family when children are older and parents need to fill an emotional hole. If you do not have children, any dog of any age is always acceptable, but stay away from its mouth when it's sleeping.

There are times I can see myself getting a dog when my children are grown. I occasionally think of that toasty, vibrating dustbuster at my feet in bed and miss the feeling. When my sister's dog, Jackson, hops into our bed while we're visiting, I pretend to be annoyed, but I secretly love it. Not all dogs smell or shed. Maybe when our kids are gone, and our caretaking tanks are not constantly empty, we might enjoy doting on a new living thing. But what if we want to travel a lot? I remember a time when my family boarded Bandit at a kennel, and when we picked him up three days later, he was hoarse and wheezing. The kennel said he'd barked nonstop for more than forty-eight hours; they had to put him in a separate part of the building to keep the other dogs from going insane. Sometimes you get a dog like that. I'm just not sure I can risk it.

Chapter 11

HOW LONG FOR A
PASSPORT?

Moving: Part 3

MY MOTHER WAS ASKING ME ON THE PHONE IF THERE WAS
any news on the apartment that she could pass on to her Bible study
group. She was in charge of texting everyone the week's prayer
requests, and I was on the list.

This group of women in their seventies and eighties had been
praying for me, Michael, and Lois ever since my mother had told
them the whole cockamamie story. I knew other things they were
praying for, too, even though I doubt I was supposed to. Transcribing
the week's prayer requests from a notebook to a group text was a task
my mother approached with the attitude I likened to my gathering
all of my freelancer receipts for my accountant the day before my
taxes were due. First of all, she texts with the pad of her middle

finger, her immaculate nails fanned out, like she's giving her iPhone a high five. It takes forever. And every once in a while, she thinks she's tapped the wrong button and lost the text, prompting a phone call to my sister or me, as if we can help from one thousand miles away. We've tried to teach her how to text on her iPad, but something is wrong with the iPad (her words). So because I hear about the labor involved in being the de facto Bible study secretary, I also hear about the issues being laid at God's feet. There is cancer. Addiction issues. Estranged family members. My apartment predicament felt like the smallest of small potatoes. But I think the story was providing some entertainment to the group. A few of the women had texted me about reading my first book, and every one of them ended her message with And we are praying for the apartment! Also, I firmly believe that God does care about seemingly unsacred details of our lives, like apartment contracts. He's capable of turning the mundane holy, as I would soon find out. In any respect, I had prayed all summer for patience, for movement, for resolution, and I was frustrated. I was happy for another group of people, especially one as faithful and persistent as this one, to intercede on my behalf for a while.

One afternoon my mother called to chat and get an update to send in her weekly group text. I'd been hesitant to talk to her about Lois, because things had stalled and I didn't have anything to report.

"I don't even want to *ask* if there's any news about the apartment. I know you don't know anything," Mom said. She sounded exasperated—at me, at Lois, I couldn't tell which. "I guess I'll tell Bible study nothing's changed."

Indeed, it had not been a great fall.

The apartment was owned by the estate of Lois's late husband.

As far as we knew, there were no relatives jockeying to inherit it. It was Lois's outright. But her attorney wanted to transfer the title to her name before signing a contract. That process turned out to be a long one, partially because it took Lois a while to find necessary paperwork, partially because the building's managing agent—essentially the real estate company that handled the building's business—moved at the speed of a garden slug, and partially because Lois's attorney seemed to have no interest in closing the deal. He took weeks to respond to emails. When Michael or our attorney managed to get him on the phone, he refused to answer simple questions. I continued checking in with Lois every couple of weeks, but she was often confused and overwhelmed. Her blood pressure was acting up. More than once she mentioned "the closing," and I had to explain that there would be a closing, of sorts, to finalize the title transfer, but that it was not a closing on the sale of the apartment. We still had to sign the contract, I told her.

"Oh yes, oh Lord. I just want this done." she said one morning. She'd been at the apartment the week before to get a wheelchair to give to her cousin. "I just can't deal with all that stuff. That apartment is such a mess. I am worried for you, I really am. I pray for you."

Join the club, I thought.

What I said was, "Thank you."

"I'm so sorry this is taking so long. I know you have the kids . . ."

"It's fine, Lois. Don't worry about us. I'll call you in a couple of weeks."

The last week of October, just before Halloween, we moved out of our apartment and into a sublet. At the end of the summer a family with four kids, who were close friends of ours, relocated to Nashville where they had a second home. They weren't yet ready to sell their apartment in the city. It had three bedrooms and was only blocks from our current place. It was recently renovated and beautifully furnished—an ideal temporary setup. We could put our stuff in storage and move in with just clothes and some of Sam's toys, and our friends would have the mortgage covered while they figured out if or when they'd sell the place. Would we even need a full year? Maybe not, we reasoned. We were so close to signing the contract. We already had preliminary plans from the architect. We'd found a contractor. We'd been preapproved for a construction loan from the bank. The title transfer would go through any day now, and we'd sign the contract.

I was uncharacteristically calm the week of the move. Knowing that it would be physically and emotionally exhausting with three children, I asked the movers to pack everything that was going to storage, which was 90 percent of our belongings. I told Michael that I could not watch the men empty our home. He'd have to do it. In the days before the movers arrived, I dismantled and gave away the kids' bunk beds and Sam's crib. Everyone slept on mattresses on the floor the final night, even my mother who had come into town to help. She fed children and put them to bed, while Michael and I took carloads of clothes and other necessities (any paperwork we might need in the coming year, sleeping bags for summer camp, ski clothes just in case) over to the sublet. I was calm, because we would be back. I wasn't sad, because it wasn't the end of our family's time in that building. There would be a brief interlude, and then we'd return. I was sure of it.

On October 27 when the movers arrived, I stayed away. A funny thing about me and moving: watching men (I've never had a female mover, although I suppose they're out there) wrap and hoist your furniture down hallways and stairs and into elevators is excruciating. It's not that I think they will damage my belong-ings. It's that the process of moving is so unpleasant, it pains me to watch perfectly nice strangers, even ones I am paying, do it for me. When I see a young man sweating and then panting, "I got it, hold, okay, okay, no, I don't, set it down," I have to look away. It is worse than watching my child kick the ball into her own goal in a soccer game or sitting through multiple shots at the doctor's office, which are both over in seconds, while moving takes hours. Seeing low-level human misery for my benefit is too much to take. I feel similarly about eating meat, something our family has tried to do less of in the past few years. Slow food advocates and the vendors at the farmer's market would argue that part of our responsibility in being educated meat eaters is that we know where our food comes from, that caring about how an animal lived and was slaughtered is important. I understand that. But I just want to pull a chicken breast out of a plastic sleeve and not think about it. I just want to arrive at my new apartment once all the furniture has made it up the freight elevator and not dwell on the unpleasantness that preceded it.

That day, every time I called Michael to check in I could barely hear him over the screaming of packing tape being pulled and snapped, pulled and snapped. Everything was moving quickly and efficiently, he said, and I was grateful. That night I went over to take a look. I knew there was still work to do before we handed over the keys. I'd need to sweep and mop the floors, patch some holes in the wall, and empty the refrigerator, which was still full of con-diments—so many condiments. I wanted to clean the oven, a job every friend told me was unnecessary when I mentioned it. But I'd really neglected it over the last few years. It was filthy; the door was opaque with rust-colored grease. And the couple who had bought our apartment was young. Newlyweds. They were exactly who we were when we bought the apartment. I wanted to hand over the cleanest, warmest, most welcoming empty home I could. I wanted them to know how much we loved it, how much it had loved us. The appliances were fourteen years old. I feared the couple would move in only to have everything break within a few months. The least I could do, I reasoned, was leave the floors, fixtures, walls, and oven racks in their most presentable state. Our scuffed, bruised little home could still be a solid place to land. Michael came with me, and after we walked through the empty apartment, our steps echoing in that awful or wonderful way that signals a beginning or a goodbye, we went to the roof. I cried a little, looking out at the lights.

"I'm getting it out now. I'm not going to cry at the closing and freak out the new owners," I said.

"It's okay if you do," he answered.

I didn't, for the record. I signed paper after paper and cracked a few jokes and told the young couple that it was such a special building, and I hoped they'd be happy there. I had to leave quickly to pick up James from school, but Michael hung around until everyone left. He told me later that the young couple walked out of the building in front of him, not knowing he was there. He said they stopped, smiled at each other with excitement, and kissed, then crossed the street holding hands.

Lois called in late November to tell me that she had an appointment at her lawyer's office the next week to sign the title transfer. Then, we thought, we can sign the contract, call it a day, and move toward closing on the apartment. Finally. It had taken four months to get the title transfer in order. On the day of Lois's meeting with her attorney, Michael emailed him to ask if he could let us know how everything went. He emailed back, "The meeting was canceled. My client cannot sign any documentation because she does not have a photo ID."

Excuse me?

How had we come this far, made this much progress, only to find out she didn't have an ID?

"I don't know how she does not have any photo ID, but if that's true, it's going to take months for her to replace it," Michael said to me on the phone. He was right. Covid had slowed everything down. Appointments to get new passports or driver's licenses were backed up and scarce. And we weren't sure if Lois had anything with her photo on it to confirm her identity, even if she could get an appointment. "I think we might be done. This might be it. We can't wait forever," Michael said.

"This is not it!" I said. "We can fix this. Surely there is a way for her to get a replacement ID quickly. I am *not* giving up right now."

If there is something you take away from these pages, let it be that God is passionately, personally concerned with every small hurt or inconvenience in your life, and you should talk to him about whatever you want, whether it is a real estate deal or a broken washing machine. What happens, though—what certainly happened to me—is that in thinking about how God cares about the humdrum business of your day, you start to fall more in love with him and less in love with the thing you started praying about in the first place. That's the best possible scenario, if for no other reason than you are a little less stressed out.

During the early months of talking to Lois, when I wanted

things to move fast, I prayed a lot. I wanted something! I'm human. And after a while I noticed a change. I began to hold the idea of the apartment loosely, as if in open hands. I began to say things like, "If it's meant to be, it will work out, and if it doesn't, then God has another apartment that we are supposed to live in." Maybe there was a family or a friend we were supposed to make in a new building, a community we'd adore, even if it came through the heartbreak of losing Lois's place. I sounded downright Zen, which is not like me.

At the same time, I did not think this lost ID was the end. It did not feel insurmountable. Maybe we'd get a nudge to walk away, but here, now, I did not sense it. I called Lois.

"Oh, honey, this is terrible. Terrible!" she said immediately after answering. I rarely got a chance to tell her it was me calling. She started talking the second she picked up, and I forever had a hard time getting a word in. "I'm telling you, I have a marriage license. I have my birth certificate. I told them I worked for the United States Postal Service! I can't get anyone to listen. They say I have to have something with my picture on it, or someone has to go vouch for me."

She told me her bag was stolen on an Amtrak train a couple of years before, and she had lost her driver's license and passport.

"And, you know, I don't travel anymore. I don't drive now. I didn't have any use for them, so I just didn't replace them," she said.

"I know, Lois. It's okay. We've been looking on the DMV website to try to figure out . . ." I stopped. At what point, Michael and I had both considered, did we cross a line with our involvement? Was it helpful for one of us to pick Lois up and take her to the DMV? Or was that manipulative, getting us closer, faster, to something we desperately wanted? We cared about Lois. We didn't want to push her. And yet we knew that this was a special situation, a once-in-a-lifetime opportunity. We knew—because, believe me, we had looked—that every other three-bedroom apartment in our neighborhood was smaller and more expensive than Lois's, and even if the kitchen cabinets and bathroom tiles were in perfect shape, I'd still want to change them, because a lot of New Yorkers have bad taste.

Lois interrupted. "And my daughter. She's helping me. She made an appointment for January for us to go to the passport office, and she will go with me to vouch for me."

That was almost two months away, but it was something.

"That's great, Lois. And in the meantime, I'll see if there's anything else you can do that would save you the trip," I said.

We could be waiting until the spring for Lois to get a new passport. Was this the end? Were we being practical or pushy? I thought about my open hands, about holding it all loosely, about letting go of this dream. And then I thought about the new Pinterest boards I'd created with photos of antique brass kitchen faucets and wallpapered powder rooms. I decided to outsource. I sat down on a bench along the park side of Fifth Avenue and called my mother.

"Hellooo," she said.

"Hi. I'm going to need your Bible study to pray for a photo ID."

Chapter 12

THE CHAPTER OF
QUESTIONABLE OPINIONS

I AM NOT WHAT YOU WOULD CALL A PEOPLE PLEASER. I AM THE opposite. In many circumstances of my early years, I've been a people agitator. A people disappointer. When faced with an opportunity to either go along with whoever is in charge to keep the peace or express my point of contention, I have been inclined toward the latter for most of my life. What happens as you get older, however, is that you have to slog through so many mandatory arguments and difficult relationships that you stop choosing optional ones. You also learn tact and how to read a room and when a dissenting voice will add to the conversation or just ruin everyone's night.

Once, about ten years ago, Michael and I had dinner with two other couples, both of whom we were, and still are, quite close with. Everyone at the table was from the Northeast except me, and the talk turned to colleges—what was worth the money, if our children would go to the same schools we went to, that sort of thing. I should note that four out of the six guests, my husband included, went to Harvard or Princeton. That's how they all knew each other. I went to a state university, a very good one, and I have a strongly held opinion about higher education that is unpopular with a lot of people I meet in New York: in this part of the country you get a lot of high-achieving children from high-achieving families who fetishize Ivy League schools. Except not every kid is going to get into those schools, obviously. And those kids who don't get in don't necessarily want to leave the cozy enclave of New England, or they want to be close to their friends and parents, or they still want a small liberal arts school that feels as special as they are. Fortunately for them, this area is positively covered in that type of school. There's Bates, Bowdoin, Bucknell, Colby, Hobart, and Hamilton, just to name a few. My nephew is at Hamilton. He plays on the soccer team. He's very happy. I'm happy for him.

My point is that before I moved to New York, I had never heard of any of those schools except Bucknell, because I knew one person who went there. In the South, I argued, there aren't a million stone-walled, wannabe prestigious liberal arts colleges dotting the landscape, so if you didn't get into a reach school—maybe it was Harvard, but maybe it was Vanderbilt—and you wanted to stay close to your friends or parents, you probably ended up at a public university like Clemson or Texas A&M. (Which *are* reach schools for some kids; everything is relative!) It doesn't mean those high school seniors aren't as smart and accomplished as the ones going to Bates. Going to a state school isn't an indictment on their intelligence. "It's practicality," I said that night at the dinner table. "Sometimes it's money. A lot of these schools give full rides to in-state kids with a 4.0. And yet y'all turn up your noses at the

University of Tennessee but think Colgate is a good school. I'm sorry, but Colgate? Who goes to *Colgate*?"

"I went to Colgate," said a calm voice from the other end of the table.

It was Kristina, who had recently married our friend Jamie. I had not yet spent enough time with Kristina to know where she'd gone to college. Kristina was a successful art dealer and, in every conversation I'd ever had with her, nothing but wise and gracious. She certainly possessed enough poise and common sense not to make the blunder I just had. I was mortified. I apologized on the spot and emailed another apology the next day, but I've never fully gotten over it. Whenever I see Kristina now, that night still comes to mind and I feel bad all over again, even though we've known each other for decades at this point, and I think she's forgiven me.

For what it's worth, the entire conversation is moot these days, the way college admissions have become so deliriously competitive. I don't think I could get into Colgate or the University of Tennessee if I were currently applying. And Michael likes to remind me that the South has its own smattering of private liberal arts schools unknown to many outside of the region: Wofford, Samford, Sewanee, Hendrix. I tried to put Davidson on that list, and he rolled his eyes and dropped his head. "Elizabeth, people know about Davidson outside of the South! Good god, Steph Curry went there."

Listen, I'm full of passionate arguments that don't hold water. But I did learn a lesson that night ten years ago. Assume, when opening your big mouth, that someone at the party went to Colgate. In other words, be nice. Recognize that everyone has different experiences even in the same circumstances. Remember that opinions aren't facts and facts aren't opinions. (Oh, how we've forgotten that one in the past couple of years.) Ask questions instead of talking nonstop. Acknowledge that you might be completely wrong in your thinking. Those rules have allowed me to let some of my more peculiar theories out of the bag and the freedom to adjust my thinking when presented with compelling discourse. If we never talk about these things, we'll never have the chance to change our minds.

So, I don't really think seventeen-year-olds should get the final word on where they go to college. Their brains are still cooking! I'm not saying they don't get a vote, just that parents should put their thumbs on the scale. If in five years my child is deciding between Swarthmore and the University of Georgia, well, you know where I stand.

As for the rest of these questionable opinions, a couple are fun, and some might send me into hiding.

OPEN KITCHENS ARE OVERRATED.

Joe, the architect working on Lois's apartment, gave us three options for how we could renovate it to suit our needs as a family of five. In the early fall, after selling our two-bedroom apartment but before closing and moving out, Michael and I had paid Joe to give us his thoughts on what it would take to make the space livable, first of all, but also reconfigure a few things. We'd need Joe's estimate and cost breakdown to get a construction loan from the bank, should we ever get to that point. He told us beforehand that he'd offer three potential plans. One would be simple, hardly moving a wall. One would be slightly more creative. And one would be pie-in-the-sky, where he could show what was possible outside of our limited imaginations.

I'll go ahead and kill the suspense and say that we picked the first, most boring option. The layout of the apartment was darn near perfect as is. We wanted to enlarge the kids' bathroom and move the washer/dryer, but for the most part, the work would be cosmetic. Joe's second option flip-flopped the dining room and Julia's bedroom, giving her a private bathroom but putting her room on the front of the building, facing the street, where we worried noise might be a problem. That was out. The third option, the pie-in-the-sky one, was intriguing. Joe had turned the galley kitchen into a laundry and mudroom—an extravagance in New York City, where most washer/dryers are stacked on top of each other in a closet—and moved the kitchen to the opposite side of the apartment, where a large bathroom had been. On his drawings we saw what every HGTV show of the past decade had told us we should want: an open kitchen with an island that spilled over to a dining area that opened into a living room. When Michael and I showed the plans to friends or family members, we would go in order. "Here is Plan A. This is what we will probably choose." And, "Here is Plan B, but we don't love how the bedroom is on the front." And, "Here is Plan C, where you can see he flipped the kitch—" Every single person, down to a one, stopped us before we could say another word. "Ooooh, *that one*," they'd say.

What is it with everybody and open kitchens?

I think open kitchens and islands are annoying. "My worst nightmare" is actually how I have described the setup to a few close friends. For years I lived in New York City apartments with stovetops the size of legal pads and dreamed of the expanse of counter space an island would afford me. It seemed so out of reach. But after two decades, I guess I've lost the lust. I adapted to cooking in a closed-off space, and now when I visit my sister or my mother or truly any other adult human outside of New York, I am more and more sure of my feelings. Our rental apartment has an open kitchen with a spacious island that butts up against the family room, and after living there for several months, I have to say it's not for me.

There is the simple fact that I don't want to look at dirty dishes from the couch. If I'm throwing a dinner party, I often leave the bulk of the mess—the Dutch oven, the casserole dish, a stack of ice cream bowls—until the morning, and I don't want it taunting me while I'm trying to relax. Ditto for my guests being able to see them from the dining table while we eat. I drop things on the floor and put them back in the bowl all the time. No one needs to be the wiser or get on my case. Multitasking is not my strong suit, which means that if I'm having a conversation with you while driving, I will miss my turn. If you're going to crowd around my kitchen island and chat with me while I cook, I'll forget to add the cheese. It is inevitable. When a friend says, "I'll just stand here and talk to you while you're finishing the salad," I think, *Please don't—for your sake, if you'd like all the ingredients included, and for my sake, sanity.* Islands, I have noticed, tend to be repositories of crap. They are only clutter free and topped with a fruit bowl in photos and before company comes. Ninety percent of the time there is a pile of mail, several mismatched socks, and the family cat taking up most of the space. Too many minutes of my day are already spent saying things like, "Put your pajamas in the hamper," and "That plate doesn't have legs, last time I checked." I don't want to add, "Guys, help me clear the *island*." And then there is the big reason that I prefer a smaller, closed kitchen: islands have barstools. And barstools invite children to sit down with their homework and interact with me. Trying to make dinner under these conditions is like being on a cooking show where the contestant has to simultaneously pull apart a rotisserie chicken and recall the lead-up to the French and Indian War.

My friends who have islands tell me I'm wrong. They say maybe I don't want my kids in the kitchen *now*, but I *will*. They say I'm in a particular phase of parenting, that my kids—at least two of them, anyway—are still relatively young and loud, that we're coming out of a rare season of too much togetherness, and that those things are coloring my opinion. "Soon they'll be teenagers, and they won't talk to you," these friends say. "They won't be around."

I may eat these words down the road, but I cannot imagine that my children will ever stop talking to me and, if they do, that it won't be a blessed relief. Just a few weeks ago, the oldest walked eight inches behind me from room to room for forty-five minutes as I washed my face, applied several layers of skin care, lotioned my limbs, got dressed, tidied up the toys in her brothers' bedroom, and folded a load of laundry. She was telling me the entire plot of a novel called *Keeper of the Lost Cities*, even though I stopped, held her precious face in my hands, and said, "I love you, but I do not care about this," more than once. Last night, while I sliced bread for dinner, my middle child sat at the island and cried through his math homework while sweeping eraser shavings onto my cutting board, where they mingled with the bread crumbs. When he was finished with his math, he wanted to read me a poem he'd written about his favorite overalls. If my children don't speak to me from the years 2024 to 2030, I'd say we are barely even. Give me a galley kitchen with a door, please.

As trusted person after trusted person in my life went gaga over Plan C, though, I started to feel insecure. I knew I didn't want an open kitchen with an island, even if it did mean I'd have less counter space. I *knew*. But no one agreed with me. Friends would tilt their heads and say, "Really? No?" And it wasn't like this was me declaring I preferred mid-rise jeans from the Gap to the high-waisted ones from Madewell everyone was raving about. This was the renovation of an apartment I planned to live in forever. This was hundreds of thousands of dollars. My confidence began to get fuzzy. So I started defending myself, first with the arguments above, but then by poking fun. "I'm weird!" I'd say. "I'll probably totally regret it! Who chooses the smaller kitchen, right? Probably a huge mistake, but, whatever, it's just how I am. Ha ha ha."

One of the last people I showed our plans to was Jeanne, Michael's aunt, who picks up James and Sam from school one day a week. She came over to drop off James around 6:30 and sat down at the island to have a beer with me while I finished cleaning up Sam's dinner dishes. (Would I enjoy this? A beer with another person while I cleaned up? Ugh, I couldn't rely on my own feelings anymore.) Somehow we had yet to show Jeanne the architect's drawings, so I handed them to her and listened as she, like everyone else, picked Plan C.

"Yeah, it's nice. I know," I said.

"That's a big space you'd have there," she said.

"You're right, but I like being alone in the kitchen. It's my territory; I can concentrate without my family's entire life up in my face. It's like an escape. I'm weird, I know. No one agrees with me. Everyone is with you. I'm being dumb."

"You know, Elizabeth, you're allowed to like what you like. You feel a certain way, and that's okay," Jeanne said.

She's right. Of course she's right. It can be that simple. I like what I like. Kitchens aren't life and death. Don't come talk to me while I'm cooking.

ATLANTIC COAST BEACHES ARE BETTER THAN GULF COAST BEACHES.

If you want to fight me on this—and believe me, I just heard the collective gasp of every one of you from Memphis, Nashville, Birmingham, and Jackson—you are going to have to go through my sister, Holland. This is her fault.

Our family, like many from the mid-South area, drove nine hours to Destin, Florida, on the panhandle for a week every summer or so. I say "or so" because, as you know, my dad did not like the beach. He burned to a crisp in the sun—we all did—and hated sitting in the heat, which meant that beach vacations were never guaranteed. A few times, my mother drove us to Destin on her own, meeting up with other moms and kids from Memphis. We always stayed at the Silver Dunes resort, a two-story condo complex right on the Gulf of Mexico. It wasn't fancy. No matter which unit we ended up in, there was almost always shag carpeting, stiff beds, and a constant waft of mildew.

Destin itself was one long, ugly concrete highway of hotel after hotel, some squatty, like Silver Dunes, some stretching dozens of floors up. It was densely developed from my earliest memories. But none of that mattered. Beyond the wall of buildings lay water that rivals anything in the Caribbean and beaches that look like snow if you didn't know better. Destin wasn't quaint. It was crowded and loud. It's just that the beaches were too good for any of us to care. One year I got so sunburned, a common occurrence no matter how much sunscreen I applied, that my mother resorted to a technique she'd clipped from a women's magazine: slathering Selsun Blue dandruff shampoo all over my body. I slept with the dried, medicated shampoo on all of my limbs and woke up exactly the same, blistered and sore, but still ran straight out to those powder-soft beaches the minute the sun came up.

In college my in-state friends vacationed at Atlantic Beach and Wrightsville Beach. My roommate, Ginger, was from Wrightsville Beach, and her parents owned a restaurant in town, so we could swing a free place to stay plus leftover, appetizer-sized meatballs and cheese dip, if we were lucky. Those trips were my first introduction to Atlantic Coast beaches. I always had fun with my friends, but in terms of my attitude toward the actual beach, you might as well have dropped Eloise into a Motel 6. Everything was inferior. The water was brown. The sand was tan and rough, not the silky Floridian ambrosia I was accustomed to. Every chance I got, I noted the discrepancies. I longed to vacation on the Gulf with my friends who had gone to Auburn and spent their school breaks down there. Developers had begun filling the sleepier parts of the panhandle east of Destin with cutesy neighborhoods like Seaside, which was used as the set on *The Truman Show*. Now you could get the beautiful beach and a sweet little pink cottage with gingerbread trim. No more shag carpeting or monstrous high-rises. What could be better?

My sister got married while I was in college. Her husband, Scott, started medical school, and my sister worked long hours as a consultant, flying back and forth from clients during the week to home on the weekends, paying the bills. They moved from West Virginia to Winston-Salem to Nashville, as Scott finished his training, and then they settled in Pawleys Island, South Carolina, a mostly vacation community on the coast. They had three sons there. After about ten years in Pawleys Island, they moved to the Charleston area, where their house is fifteen or twenty minutes, depending on traffic, from Sullivan's Island and Isle of Palms.

I always tell people who aren't very familiar with the South that there is more than one. There is the South where I am from: Memphis, which is shoved so far down into the Southwest corner of the state of Tennessee that it is, culturally and geographically, more part of Mississippi and Arkansas than the booming, celebrity-filled Nashville or the hills and mountains of Chattanooga or Knoxville. My South is muddy and flat, full of cotton and soybean fields. Our music is blues. Our tea is not usually sweet. We have the mighty Mississippi River but no ocean anywhere close. The Carolinas are a completely different animal: you have mountains and beaches within a few hours' drive, and girls and boys I met in college grew up listening to The Embers and knowing how to shag. I loved it, but it wasn't home. The longer I've lived in New York, the stronger my attachment to Memphis and the Deep South has become, because I don't want to lose that part of myself. I hold on tightly to my friends who still live there, yes, but also to specific barbecue restaurants and old buildings and even the vacations I took as a child to the Gulf Coast. I could never love a different South than my South because there was only so much room in my heart.

Holland and I look alike. People think we are twins, even though her darker auburn hair and softer face favor my mother, and I have my father's build and his green eyes. I always say it's not that we look identical; it's that we don't look similar to anyone else but each other. We are reddish haired and freckled and have the same jelly bean–shaped nostrils. It thrills me when people know we're sisters, because Holland is strikingly pretty and has an easy laugh. It only bothers me a bit when everyone assumes I'm older. (She is, by almost four years.) We fought like wild hyenas as kids but have settled into similar patterns as adults. We both prize self-sufficiency and humor. We say "I love you" at the end of phone conversations only on birthdays, and yet we never doubt the other's utter devotion. When I left for a month-long trip to serve at a youth camp in Canada the summer after I graduated from high school, Holland gave me a book she'd recently read and loved—*Snow Falling on Cedars* by David Guterson—and every forty or fifty pages, she'd left a sticky note with a funny message or a word of encouragement. Her love is always quiet and steady.

One thing we don't share is an over-romanticization of Memphis. Holland enjoyed her childhood just fine, but when she moved to North Carolina for college, she moved on. She fell in love with a different South and never looked back. It's one of my favorite qualities of hers, the ability to thrive in new circumstances without making a big fuss about it. I write entire books about my changing identities. She just gets on with enjoying her life and doesn't care what anyone thinks about her business. The thing is, her business became the rest of the family's business, because she started hosting a lot of holidays. Soon enough, my parents and my kids and Michael and I were spending more and more time in Charleston and less and less time in Memphis. If we wanted to rent a beach house for a week in the summer, it made sense to do it near Holland. We became Atlantic Coast beach people.

It's easy to say that you love what those you love also love. I've fallen for the beaches in South Carolina because I love my sister and her life there; her enthusiasm rubs off. But it's also the wildness of the place. Unlike the skinny strip of sand between the condos and the water on the Gulf Coast, the beaches of Isle of Palms or Kiawah or Sullivan's are so vast, my children become specks in the distance within minutes. When the tide goes out, it feels like you could walk to the horizon. The water isn't blue, but it's earnest, formidable. Nothing is tame or precious on the Atlantic Coast.

The wind is usually too strong for an umbrella, but it also keeps you comfortable, even on the hottest days. My kids drag driftwood and bleached, papery reeds across the sand to make borders for houses or flags for castles. Unless you are near Myrtle Beach, there are few high-rises, just dunes with grass sprouting from them, like hairy warts along the shore. Living in the Northeast, I've now spent time on Block Island, off the coast of Rhode Island, on Cape Cod, and even in the Hamptons. The water at all of those beaches is too cold. One part of my Southern upbringing I'll never escape is my need for the ocean to be just above the temperature of matzo ball soup. (Also, Cape Cod has sharks.) Otherwise, though, all of those beaches have an untamed quality that appeals to me. They're beautiful because they're rough around the edges.

When Sam was just six months old, Allegiant Air began flying between Newark, New Jersey, and Destin, Florida, for about thirty-nine dollars a ticket. It was as if an old boyfriend had come calling. My nostalgia tentacles buzzed. I couldn't wait to show my kids the Emerald Coast, as they call it, of my childhood. We booked a condo halfway between Destin and Panama City, on the stretch of highway known as 30A, where everyone from my part of the South now vacationed. I purposefully picked a condo complex that reminded me of Silver Dunes, for old times' sake. The inside of our rental was renovated, but the exterior was a nondescript stucco low-rise with a grassy courtyard and a pool that fronted the beach. And the beach did not disappoint. It was as soft and pearly as ever. The water was blue and calm. Canvas beach chairs with matching umbrellas appeared in neat rows every morning, and we sat and dug and swam and played and had a magical vacation. But that stretch of highway is different from when I was growing up. It's packed with new neighborhoods, each one like a stylized section of Disney World. This one is all-white and Mediterranean in feel. This one has a Tudor village vibe. This one is all pastels. Everything is stunning. It really is. I'm sure we will go back at some point. But I've decided, after all this time, that given the choice, I prefer wild.

I'M PRETTY SURE I'D BE JUST AS SATISFIED IN LIFE WITHOUT KIDS. (YES, I KNOW I HAVE THREE OF THEM—TWO OF WHOM CAN READ.)

There is a story that was told over and over in our household when I was growing up, about the origins of our nuclear family. My mother would often mention it just as my father was praising one of my sister's or my accomplishments. "And this," she'd say, laughing, "from the man who didn't want children."

As the tale goes, my father did not want to get married, either. But I put less stock in that notion. Plenty of men in their twenties don't think they want to get married, until they do. My father had some help in his decision—a dentist in Knoxville who my mother started dating when my father was taking too long making up his mind about marriage. One day she flew back to Memphis from Knoxville, and my father picked her up at the airport with a bunch of diamonds on loan from the local jeweler. He told her to pick one for her engagement ring. She picked the biggest.

He was still not convinced about children—and then my mother got pregnant with my sister. Neither of them ever clearly confessed to how that happened, although my sister and I have our suspicions. But when Holland was born, a fire was lit. "You would have thought he was the only man in that hospital to ever have a child," my mother always said. When I came along he insisted on a different hospital, one where fathers were allowed in the delivery room. He'd had to wait outside during my mother's labor with Holland, and he wasn't missing a minute, ever again.

He wasn't a natural at parenting. He was short-tempered and exasperated by us and constantly willing us to mature, to enjoy things he enjoyed, like Mozart and snapper and *The Day the Earth Stood Still.* Once when we were in Memphis, he took me to Goldsmith's department store, now long gone, and sat me on the display case in the beauty department while he sampled colognes. "How does this one smell?" he asked, spritzing it in front of my face. "Like a gin and tonic," I answered. The saleswoman nearly fainted.

He was an exceptional dad. I've heard the story about him not wanting kids a thousand times, and it never makes me feel unloved or insecure, because my lived experience told me otherwise. When my sister and I were small, we rarely went to bed with wet hair after a bath, or let it air dry as we ran down the hallway between our rooms in the evening. Once toweled off, we would sit on the floor at the foot of my parents' bed while my father would blow-dry our hair. "Go let your dad blow-dry it pretty," is the exact phrase my mother used. My father knew his way around a hair dryer. He liked to blow-dry his own fine, slightly wavy hair, and he relied on a Conair dryer the size of a Walkman that came with an attached brush that he ran over his head with one hand while smoothing the surface with the other. This Conair two-in-one model went off the market before my father's zeal waned, so when his broke, he would take it apart and rewire it to work again. For my sister and me, he would use a separate hairbrush, though, twisting and pulling it down our backs as he held my mother's hair dryer close to our skulls. "There, look at you. Beautiful!" he'd say as he finished, running his hands over our heads and patting the back of our flannel nightgowns.

.I remind myself often: My dad claimed he didn't want to be a dad. And I never felt anything but adored.

Ann Patchett wrote a wonderful essay in her most recent collection titled "There Are No Children Here," in which she recounts all of the situations when a person has pushed back on her expressed desire not to have children. When I read about these people saying things like, "Your husband is considerably older than you are. Chances are you'll be alone at the end of your life. Don't you worry about that?" I am dumbstruck. (There are so, so many examples of this bald-faced busybodiness; I'm shocked Ann Patchett never smacked anyone.) Maybe I shouldn't be surprised by the way people assume their opinions are canon, that surely we are all on the same page when it comes to a woman wanting kids, but I am. I could imagine a lovely, full life without children.

This is easy for me to say now that I have them. I realize this. Once you've been lucky enough to get pregnant, carry children to term, and have uncomplicated pregnancies—more than once, no less—you don't start talking about how nice it would be if you and your husband could instead be sitting, undisturbed, on an adults-only beach. My dad had it right, actually. Declare that you don't want children on the front end. Then, when the wind shifts, you embrace your good fortune and forget all earlier misjudgments. In my case, I'm second-guessing my earlier assumptions that motherhood was inevitable and that I'd be good at it. And when the wind shifts in that scenario, even imperceptibly, even only on occasion, you are supposed to ignore it.

But it seems to me that there are three groups of people in this world when it comes to having children: those who know definitively that it's not for them; those who know definitively that it is; and those who assume they are in the second group, due to societal expectations or the ignorance of youth, but realize after the fact that they could be happy either way yet now can't say anything, because the kids are listening. I'm very much in awe of the first two groups, and I think there are more of us than we realize in the last. That's all. I love my kids; I also dream of an empty nest. Am I the only one who wants to talk about it? Yesterday a friend emailed me—it happens to be December while I'm writing this—remarking about how lucky I was to still have little kids at Christmas. "When they're grown, it just isn't that much fun," she wrote, adding that she was giving her twentysomething daughter a couch. I long to give my child a couch. My most recent purchase was a roll-up, rainbow silicone piano that cost sixty dollars at the Museum of Modern Art gift shop.

Like my dad, I'm not what the world would consider a natural in the parenting department. And that has its upsides. I'm not patient or particularly nurturing, and I've never once cooed that I wanted to "bottle up" anything about my children. I tend to enjoy them most when they are being independent or funny, because those are traits I like. However, no one can accuse me of raising children who've been told their whole lives that they are special and deserving of every good thing. My children are very aware that they are not the center of my attention, much less the universe. I can only imagine their college professors will thank me. There is a temptation, though, to exalt the hands-off, nobody's-special, burn-it-all-down philosophy over the every-moment-is-a-blessing one, and that's a mistake. Neither will save us.

I actually think looking at our children as our neighbors, in the biblical sense, is the best option. We are supposed to love and serve our neighbors and to give them the shirt off our back if they are in need. We're supposed to look out for the ones who are most vulnerable and protect them. We are supposed to feed them and welcome them into our homes, even if they are strangers or are antagonistic toward us, which, at certain points in parenting, is exactly how I'd describe children. The less I look at my kids as some sort of extension of myself or project to be conquered, and the more I see them as neighbors (strange, antagonistic neighbors) whom I am to serve without expectation of thanks, the more everything makes sense.

There have been many surprises in middle age, but a big one has been that the bell curve of marriage, work, and parenthood is completely upside-down from what I expected. From my favorite books, movies, and couples I managed to pay attention to in adolescence, it appeared that a lust for my young husband and for moving up the editorial ranks of different publications would wane with time as my devotion to my children grew. And, well, that hasn't happened. Marriage has gotten better and better, and I now write with more pleasure and freedom than I ever have. There is an argument to be made that those improvements are dependent on my life as it's panned out, with kids. I'm a more forgiving and charitable partner because I've been humbled by motherhood. Having children has certainly provided content for my work. All true. But I can also imagine a life of reading, traveling, and researching, of not keeping track of time. I follow the work of other writers, those without children, and am jealous of the ability to create organically, without the specter of school pickup hanging over them. Of course, those child-free writers have their own obligations: aging parents and needy friends and volunteer commitments. Few of us are on the exact highway we imagined.

Actually, from everything I've read, it sounds like Ann Patchett is. Good for her.

I am happy here with my crazy neighbors. I could also have been happy without them. I think it's okay to say that.

I DON'T WANT TO GO TO THERAPY. DO I HAVE TO?

I'd like to state up front that cataloging a list of reasons why you don't want to go to therapy is a surefire way for people to point out why you need to go to therapy. I'm aware. I'm also aware that for too long—especially in churchy circles that I come from—seeing a therapist or taking medication related to mental health carried a stigma. But, geez, okay, I just need to say that it seems to me the pendulum has swung halfway, if not fully, in the other direction, and now there is a chorus of voices in my life (and by life, I mean Instagram) not-so-gently implying that everyone should be in therapy, and if I am not, I am living a life of darkness, unaware of the joy and fulfillment that could be mine. Am I exaggerating? Yes. I exaggerate everything. But case in point: of the handful of podcasts I listen to regularly, all but one have ads for BetterHelp, an online therapy service that promises to match me with a therapist that I can speak to on the phone, on a video chat, with or without the camera on, with a bag over my head, any way I want as long as I talk to someone within forty-eight hours. When I listen to a podcast with a Christian angle, I get ads for Faithful Counseling, which is the same—except when I'm hiding under a bag, the Holy Spirit can still see me.

The *New York Times* ran an opinion piece in October 2022

titled, "Why Do People Think Going to Therapy Makes You a Good Person?" The author, Mychal Denzel Smith, wrote that more and more people are going to therapy—but perhaps for no other reason than the nebulous feeling that they *should*. My thoughts exactly. Smith applauds the idea that therapy has become less stigmatized, and yet he wrote, "I've started to wonder if there's a flip side to this openness, a new form of judgment that has broken down into a too-simple binary: In therapy, good; not in therapy, bad."[1]

There's truth to that. I don't need to go to therapy to know it can be wonderful; I've seen its positive effects in the lives of people I love.

Also, I am not an idiot. I write nonfiction essay collections, something you have to be an itsy bit of a narcissist to take on. I have spent years of my life navel-gazing, writing about beliefs and changes of heart and complicated relationships, all to make sense of why I am the way I am and what needs work. Here, I'll tell you. With my hypothetical therapist, I would probably need to start with my obsession with self-sufficiency, how my family prized taking care of your own business and not being needy, and how all of my life I've been judgmental of people who show weakness. This is why it took me so very long to make the decision to see my hypothetical therapist in the first place. Next, I would want to talk about how anger is such a comfortable emotion for me, how I justify it, and how I still don't feel like I have a hold on it, even after years of trying. I'd ask Eileen (my hypothetical therapist's name is Eileen) if anger can be a symptom of depression. I might wonder

---

1. Mychal Denzel Smith, "Why Do People Think Going to Therapy Makes You a Good Person?," *New York Times*, October 11, 2022, https://www.nytimes.com/2022/10/11/opinion/therapy-america.html.

how it's possible that I, someone who is the life of the party, who is so strong-willed and confident, who loves people and conversation and laughter, could really be depressed. Doesn't it seem weird? And yet there are times when I think I mask a sense of despair and loss of control by lashing out. Only I do it solely with those closest to me, so that outsiders are incredulous. I'm so fun, absolutely all of the time! Those are the things I'd probably need to address.

Look, I'm such a control freak that *I'm pretending to know what my hypothetical therapist would suggest we need to talk about*. I know my issues. Trust me, *I know*.

I'm not saying therapy wouldn't help.

What I am saying is that no one really talks about the cost-benefit analysis. And that's where I get stuck. Insurance probably covers part of the cost of therapy, yet that certainly isn't a given. But overall, therapy costs money. Money I have, a great privilege. Yet again I have plenty of things I could and should spend money on that would improve my life. Is therapy beneficial enough that it justifies the expense? Of this I'm unsure. "It's self-care," people tell me. For some people it is much more than that. But for many of us, myself included, yes, it's self-care. Well, so are massages, and I don't pay for those once a week.

Also, time. Please do not tell me that finding the right therapist is like dating. That's a terrible selling point. You're saying that I might spend hours and hundreds of dollars—not to mention the cost of getting a babysitter, missing work, and the inevitable, nervous sweating-through of my clothes in the hour leading up to the meeting—only for it to be awkward or boring, or she's never watched *The Americans*, which is potentially unforgivable, and I have to start all over again? I do not want to date. I do not have time to date. If it were a matter of life or death, yes. If I were feeling suicidal or in a deep depression, worth it. But if not? No. People say, "But you shouldn't wait until you are in a crisis! You need to go to therapy before the crisis, so when you hit the crisis, you are better equipped to handle it." Makes perfect sense. My counterargument is, What if it's four more years until I hit a crisis? That's a lot of time and money spent on a professional in the meantime. It is also worth noting that therapists are swamped these days; anxiety among teenagers has skyrocketed, and the pandemic has left people in tatters. If we are triaging patients, surely I should go to the back of the line.

Individuals spend their time and money in wildly different ways. There are many of you out there who think sacrificing both for therapy is paramount. For me, spending money on childcare so that I can sit in a quiet library and write these pages is all the self-care I need. I'd give almost everything I have, give up all my money and free time, for this. For me, writing trumps therapy. Maybe it is therapy. I have friends who are like sisters who hold me accountable, talk me off the proverbial ledge, and walk through dark days with me. A couple of them *are* trained counselors. We have a group Marco Polo, where I recently cried to them from a Dairy Queen bathroom. It's not like I'm suppressing my feelings. Who says I need more than what we offer each other? For free?

Smith also made this point in the *New York Times* article: "Therapy can offer a pathway toward understanding [the self], but it can also overshadow the idea of healing in community."

Would it be the worst thing in the world if I waited? Until I have more time? I'm not in crisis. I'm quite content, outside of that day at Dairy Queen. If I have a few hours, I'd really rather get a massage.

I'd like to put it off until my sixties. Maybe retirement. Then I'll find Eileen, and we'll have so much to talk about—my rich, full, tiring life. All the accomplishments I've had and terrible mistakes I've made. I will call my grown children and apologize, even though I apologize all the time now, but there will be new stuff to atone for. Maybe I'll get a fresh spark in my marriage after addressing a hurt I didn't realize I was carrying—or that he was. I'll say to my therapist, "I should have done this years ago." And it will be true. And also perfectly fine that I didn't.

Chapter 13

MIDDLE SCHOOL
IS AWESOME

THERE IS A SAYING I'VE HEARD OVER AND OVER IN MY YEARS as a parent: "Little kids, little problems. Big kids, big problems." It is almost always said in a slightly condescending way, from a parent of teenagers to a parent of toddlers, as a gentle reminder that the parent of older children has it harder, because parenting, lest you forget, is a contest. I've said it that way. I've been patronizing toward friends with a single baby. *Ha! Talk to me in a few years. Little kids, little problems. Big kids, big problems. More kids, more problems*, I imply.

As I write this my oldest child, my daughter, is in middle school. Sixth grade. She's not *big* big. She's medium big. We still have miles to go with unrequited love and college admissions essays. The child does not yet have a phone, the source of the biggest of big problems, if I'm to believe all the articles. But as a woman who is simultaneously parenting a middle schooler and a preschooler, I will take middle school any day of the week. The bigger problems are more interesting. The payout is richer.

I'm just telling you this in case you're dreading it.

Think about coming to the end of a dispute with a toddler. What do you get? Pants? A final bite of salami? The trucks in the basket? Not to underestimate the satisfaction of getting two legs through separate holes in underwear, but the denouement, so to speak, is blandly getting on with your day. And the toddler will need to be reminded again in exactly twenty-four hours how to put underwear on. Not only is the lesson kind of boring, but it doesn't stick. Contrast that with having an argument with a middle schooler. Oh, you will *crave* something as simple as underwear. You will maybe wish you had a pair of underwear handy to pull over your head, over hers, so that her complaints about her friends or her homework or you (usually you) will be muffled into oblivion. There will be no clear-cut solutions, and you'll be exhausted and angry, and it will feel so, so personal.

And yet! I have found that most—not all, but most—of the time, my child comes away with an emotional skill, a little pebble she can carry around and build on. She's learned that there comes a point in an argument with me when it's best for her to retreat to her room and write down her grievances rather than continue to yell them. She often comes back into the kitchen dramatically waving a stack of loose-leaf paper like it's the 95 Theses, but as a writer who does her best communicating via pen/fingers, I could not be more proud. One evening last week, around 9 p.m., we entered what I like to call the Vortex of Nonsensical Angst, which rolls in a few times a month and involves my daughter alternately barking at me and tearing up over a turmoil she cannot articulate. Interrupting the VoNA with a rational explanation is met with door slamming and calls for your removal.

Eventually, in our recent situation, Julia pinpointed that what she was feeling was guilt over a minor incident earlier in the day. She called the person involved to talk it through. But she did not feel better. So then we discussed shame and condemnation and how we often don't forgive ourselves even when others have. Even when God has. We stay bogged down in shame rather than walking free.

More than once, before we got to the gratifying ending, I wanted to:

- go to bed
- drink gin straight from the bottle
- stick my head in the toilet
- sob

Still, again, when all is said and done, I will take that kind of parenting over potty training eight ways 'til Sunday.

And inevitably, when I am dealing with a middle school problem, there is a spark of recognition in me.

I remember what that's like.

I had something similar happen to me.

I know what might help.

I wonder if this is precisely why most parents dread their kids entering middle school—because they remember it, and it was terrible. (Although I do think middle school has become sort of a cartoon of itself. It's the easy butt of every joke. I remember feeling vastly more insecure and left out in high school.) I don't recall middle school being so bad. My mother once said, "Those were the years when I began to get on my knees every morning and pray to make it through," so, clearly, we have conflicting accounts of that time. Perhaps I have selective amnesia about the rough patches.

What I recall, though, is that I was physically and socially immature, which spared me a lot of the confusing hormonal swings and heartache. I did not start my period until I was sixteen. I went to an all-girls school; boys were not a distraction during the day. I did have braces, but everyone had braces. There is a photo of my best friends and me at a coed dance in sixth grade. I am wearing a teal, ankle-length, long-sleeved, turtleneck, A-line dress. My hair is hot-rolled and bouncy, pulled into a half-back. Hallie is wearing a pleated, full-length skirt, collared blouse, chunky cardigan sweater (buttoned all the way), and gold costume jewelry that her mother offered while we were all getting ready at her house. Murff is wearing a full-length denim skirt and similarly chaste knit cardigan, the buttons of which look like they were molded from primary-colored modeling clay. Blair: another skirt to the ankle, turtleneck, and floral cardigan. We looked like we were engaging in *Golden Girls* cosplay, if everyone was Rose.

Here's what I do remember about middle school, and what my mother was probably praying about: I got in trouble a lot with teachers. I was a smart aleck. I had beefs.

In fifth grade—technically not middle school, but I was warming up—I timed our teacher, Miss Spencer, while she was dressing us down over some incident. She talked to us about our behavior as we sat in a semicircle on a rug in front of her chair. Everyone's eyes were on Miss Spencer. My eyes were on the clock. When Miss Spencer finished and asked if anyone had questions, I raised my hand.

"Yes, Elizabeth?"

"That lecture was eighteen minutes long. Congratulations," I said.

In sixth grade I had a religion teacher who asked the class to keep journals. For one assignment she wanted us to take them home and write about our fears. The next day she would collect the journals, read our entries, and grade them. I thought this was bogus. If she wanted us to be vulnerable and honest, she should give us privacy, I said. She did not agree. So I wrote my journal entry in ubba bubba language, which, if you are unfamiliar, is where you add *ubba bubba* to every consonant in a word and leave the vowels alone. For example: bubba bubba rubba bubba a tubba bubba spells "brat." Ubba bubba language didn't exactly take the Enigma machine to decode. My religion teacher could have figured it out pretty quickly. Maybe she did, but she wanted to make an example out of me. She demanded I translate my entry for her to read. I refused. My parents were summoned to the principal's office, and we had a meeting about my little insurrection. It wasn't the first (or last) time I went to the principal's office for being a pain in the neck (come to think of it, I believe I was once sent there for calling a teacher that exact thing). And usually, my parents were firmly with the administration. But they took my side in the religion journal case. Years later my mother said, "It was the one time I thought the school went too far with you."

In seventh grade, when our English teacher told us that she'd decided to cancel a planned quiz, I asked her, "Are you being nice because you're dying?" She asked if my parents ever taught me manners.

My problem was not that I didn't respect authority. On the contrary, I had a Southern child's deep-seated reverence for my elders and, despite the above statement, first-rate manners. It was and continues to be my personality to (1) make a joke in tense circumstances, (2) have the last word, even better if it's funny, and (3) take a righteous stand when I feel I or my classmates have been treated unfairly. Middle school was when I began to wield these traits with fervor, and for a while I swung too hard and broke a lot of things. Over time, though, I learned to thread the needle, to sharpen my skills. There is rarely a time when having to have the last word is a boon, but the others? Well, they have come in handy. Especially in parenting. A few days before the Thanksgiving break this year, Julia came home irate over the way a teacher had treated a couple of students in her class. Some kids had been minorly disruptive, and the teacher was harsh, and Julia—who was not even involved—wanted to fight back. My first instinct was to say, "Not your battle. Be quiet. Behave." And then it dawned on me: subba bubba hubba bubba e i subba bubba mubba bubba e.

She is me.

(She is I?)

She is me.

She was taking up a crusade over a perceived mistreatment, and I needed to let her. Maybe offer assistance. Be the silent guardrail in case she went too far. My mother gave me up to God in middle school, because I was brash and volatile and stubborn, and she was gentle and nonconfrontational and fed up. Maybe my similarities to my own daughter were the keys to enjoying these years. Maybe my experiences could shape hers.

The funny thing is, when I tell Julia about my gaffes and rebellions in middle school, she looks at me like I am a puppy who just tinkled on the carpet. She is at a huge public middle school in New York City, not a small Episcopal school where you have hymn sings in morning chapel. At her school there are real, no-joke fights in the recess yard a few times a year. There is bad language and bad behavior that would have made my toenails curl as a girl in Memphis in 1989. Those kids she was defending *miiight* have smashed a school-issued iPad. She is in a thick stew of urban tween humanity day in, day out. And I love it. I love it all. Other parents might think I'm crazy, but the fact that my child's middle school experience is wholly unlike mine is one of the things I love most about it. It's a gift. Let me explain.

Despite the fact that Michael and I both went to private, single-sex schools from preschool through high school, we are now committed public school people. One inescapable reason, which I have written about before but need to continually be honest about, is that private schools in New York City cost around $50,000 a year. So. We are rich, comparatively, to many of our neighbors, but we aren't that rich. Does it make the decision to go to public school in the city easy? Yes and no. Plenty of folks move to the suburbs for what they consider better public school systems, and we could have done that, but I've also said this so many times I might as well tattoo it on my forehead: if I want to live a suburban life, I'll move to Mount Pleasant, South Carolina, and live near my sister or to Memphis and live down the street from the friends I grew up with. I live in New York City because I like New York City. I do not fancy a train ride into town. Public schools are free. We have three kids. The math makes sense.

Now, the public school system in New York City has a lot of problems. It is highly racially segregated, with school zones and funding knotted up with real estate, making wealthier neighborhood schools whiter and better resourced. You can go down a long and winding rabbit hole on the inequalities with standardized testing for high schools and the hot debate surrounding those admissions. It's a mess, and there are no easy answers. We as a family are not doing public school perfectly. My older children did not attend our zoned school but instead got spots through a lottery at another neighborhood school a few blocks away, which had better test scores. Was it amazing? Some years it was. Some years a kid had a teacher who was meh, and the year was hard. Some years there was a pandemic! (Although New York City schools were open far more than public schools in other major cities, even more than some private schools in our city, and I don't think the Department of Education got enough credit for that. I mean, it was still a hellfire, don't get me wrong, but I think our schools did okay.)

I am not going to lie and say my children are getting, from a purely academic standpoint, as stellar an education as they would get in private school. No way. Their uniformly excellent teachers and principals are not miracle workers. They cannot overcome the challenge of class size or the fact that they do not get to cherry-pick their students.

The reason Michael and I send them to public school is because it is a baseline way to immerse ourselves in a community that is supposed to, even if it does it imperfectly, reflect the makeup of the city. This is one of the best ways we, as a family, can think of to commit to loving our city. I'm not saying it's *the* best or only way. Plenty of people love New York City and serve it generously and make other choices. Left to our own devices, however, I know that we will seek out community with people who look and act and think like we do. If the issues of food insecurity or mass transportation delays or navigating the educational system with a disability don't touch you on a daily basis, you will see it play out in the lives of kids in public school. I'm not even that involved in my kids' schools. In a sense, enrolling my kids in public school is the absolute least I can do, the laziest action I can take, to have my eyes opened by my community. Proximity, even if proximity is all you can muster, changes you. It has changed my kids, which is exactly why they are where they are.

Being in the public schools has made me pay more attention to local politics, because I have an issue I care about, one that affects not just my children but a million children in New York. I am forced to have an open mind about policies and solutions that might be neutral, or even slightly negative, for our family but benefit a larger group. It makes sense to us to be involved in the system—no matter how infuriating at times—that is touching the lives of the over-whelming majority of families in the city.

Julia has come home with stories about a teacher challenging her beliefs during a lesson about world religions or teaching her something that directly conflicts with what the Bible tells us. Okay! I'd rather her wrestle with those questions while she is young and still thinks I'm smart. Plus, I get to practice putting my beliefs into words and forming concise arguments along with her. I need the lessons as much as she does. Do I worry she's a sacrificial lamb in a chaotic system? Eh, not really. She's old enough to learn that her needs occasionally get sidelined for more urgent ones, that she might spend a period helping a classmate instead of advancing her own project. She's not living through a famine or war. Other parents have said to me, "But why should my child be the one to miss out on instruction or attention, while the school deals with all these other problems?" To which I say: "Why not your child? Whose child instead?"

Do I worry that Julia isn't on a track to a prestigious college? I used to. If I'm honest, I still do, but rarely. The potential triumph of telling people where your kid goes to college is hard to unhand, and I understand that being la-di-da about academics is a bridge too far for some parents. I don't know, though. Will today's middle schoolers still see secondary education the way we did? If the cost of it continues to be just south of bonkerstown, will more of them make a different choice? All I know is that releasing certain expectations and entitlements has been healthy for me and, by extension, my kids. Some public high schools in New York are cutthroat and full of high-achieving brainiacs who end up in all kinds of prestigious colleges. Maybe my kids will end up there. I'm just trying not to make it a singular focus.

One of my favorite things about middle school, though, is that it is the age when many children in New York City start going places on their own. Independence is a godsend. I have three children at three different schools. Unfortunately, there are only two parents. So the fact that one child goes to school and comes home by herself is not just novel but life-changing. It eliminates the need for me to bring her with me to her brother's preschool, which starts ten minutes earlier than her school, or else drop her off twenty minutes before the doors open. Most mornings Julia waves goodbye to us all before finishing her breakfast in peace, cleaning up her dishes, packing her backpack, and leaving the apartment last. In our old place, Julia was so close to her middle school—three blocks north, an avenue and a half west—that she did not qualify for a free MetroCard that the Department of Education gives to students to commute on the bus or subway. She walked.

Our rented apartment is ten blocks away, so she now has a MetroCard. Her public middle school is the biggest in our district, and there are so many kids commuting home in the same direction that the drivers pull two or three empty M11 city buses up to the school every day at 3 p.m. She can get to and from youth group or basketball practice or her many, many orthodontist appointments without my help. I can't overstate how divine it is. For all of us. Didn't I feel exhilarated when I got to roam my suburban neighborhood, alone, as a kid? And I couldn't even bike as far as a TCBY, much less have bodegas on every corner that will make you a perfect bacon, egg, and cheese. Honestly, my kid has it so much better than I ever did.

When Michael was growing up in the city in the 1980s, he went places on his own at a much younger age than Julia. Any time we walk down Park Avenue, he'll point to buildings and mention which school friend lived here or there and how he'd wander into the lobby to ask if so-and-so could play.

"That's where Stony Douglass lived," he'll say. "And that's where Stony Moulton lived. I had never eaten peanut butter and jelly until I went to Stony Moulton's house." (The fact that Michael knew two kids named Stony really tells you everything you need to know about the Upper East Side of Manhattan.)

Even taking into account the uptick in crime since the pandemic, New York City streets are still vastly safer now than they were in the eighties. Once, when he was about Julia's age, Michael got pushed around on his way to school by some teenagers looking for cash. Did his mother freak out and start walking him to school every morning? Nope. From then on, she tucked a five-dollar bill into his sock. "Mugging money," she told him. Hand it over and get to school on time. This is the stock my children come from.

I look at my oldest child every morning when she walks into the kitchen. She has my long legs that stick out of whatever over-sized T-shirt she's been sleeping in. Her hair is the truest strawberry blonde I've ever seen; when she was little, it looked pink. She is too beautiful for middle school. Even with braces. She tried and made the basketball team even though she'd never played before. She calls her grandmother, unasked, from her watch on her walk home from school, because she knows my mother worries about her. She lays out her clothes the night before. She babysits her brothers. Other parents trust her with their children. She is so capable that it is hard, at times, not to rely on her too much. She also has a tongue that could cut glass. But she's learning to use it for good, years before I ever did. These are the things I want her to remember about middle school. That it wasn't a throwaway time we all wish we could wipe from our lives. It was when she began to grow up, test the waters, and—sorry, but it's true—live a more interesting life.

That night around Thanksgiving, when the subba bubba hubba bubba i tubba bubba really hit the fan, and Julia was screaming in our kitchen at me, at Michael, at the world, my mother was in town for the upcoming holiday and heard it all. When things calmed down, my mother turned to me with a look of compassion and not a small bit of vindication. "Well, you got a lot worse than that as you got older," she said casually. I have bigger people and bigger problems to look forward to, I know. All the more reason to enjoy middle school while I can.

Chapter 14

LORD, MAKE ME
A SPLEEN

AT SOME POINT MOST PARENTS HAVE DONE THE NOW-FAMILIAR
is-it-a-cold-or-is-it-Covid song and dance. I have been this parent
many times over the past couple of years. I've created alternate plots
that make absolutely no sense rather than face the more obvious
answer that my child is sick and can't go to school. One of the
first times I began playing that game of denial ("Could it be aller-
gies that up until this point he has never had? Strep? Yes? Please?
Ooooh, what we wouldn't give for seasonal hay fever"), I heard
a faint ding in the back of my brain. Why did this feel familiar?
When had I done this before?

Ah. Lice. I had done this about lice.

I'm not equating lice with Covid, far from it. I'm only saying
that this desperate leap to less-plausible-but-more-treatable scenarios
isn't new. I've come up with a dozen reasons my child might have a
fever (because, truly, the possibilities are endless), and I've also knelt

in front of my child who has a red rash down the back of her neck and is scratching her head like she's a beagle and said, "I think it might be a reaction from the new laundry detergent."

Because once you confirm you have lice in your household, it really cramps your style. Kids can't go to school, your friends regard you as a pariah, and treating lice is expensive. Sure, you can do one of the homemade remedies, like putting olive oil on your head and sleeping in a turban, but I'm of the firm belief that the only thing that works is physically removing every minuscule, dishwater-colored egg from every strand of hair with a tight-tooth, metal lice comb. In case you've somehow escaped this scourge in your household, you may not know that there is a cottage industry of lice-removal experts who will do the job for you. In New York, where the dominant chain is a place called Lice Enders, they know they can charge a fortune of tired parents who just want their kids to go back to school, and they do. A plain-spoken technician once quoted me $900 to comb through my hair and that of two of my children. Nine hundred dollars. I ended up doing the kids myself and paying for someone to double-check my work and treat me (a bargain at $400).

The second time my family got lice, I did not waste time trying to convince myself that my children had both, overnight, developed severe scalp psoriasis. I knew what it was. I saw the eggs immediately. Unfortunately, by the time I confirmed that Julia and James were both infected, it was almost dinnertime the night before we were supposed to fly to North Carolina to stay at my friend Murff's mountain vacation home with four other families. All in all, there would be eleven kids sleeping in a bunk room and rubbing their heads all over each other. A quick at-home comb-through wasn't going to cut it. This was in fall 2019, still pre-Covid, which meant that the worst thing you could bring into a crowded home full of children was, still, actually, lice. If we were going to show up at the house in the mountains, I needed to at least assure my friends that a certified lice remover had cleared us. All of the salons were closed. We had flights out immediately after school the next day. I could keep the kids home from school and take them to Lice Enders, or I could call an *even more expensive* service to make a house call before bedtime.

The technician arrived at 8 p.m., so, already, we weren't doing great. I asked her to check Sam first so that he could go to bed. I held him in my lap while she squirted oil onto his scalp and combed through the few white-blonde tufts on his head. He was lice-free. Michael went to put him in his crib while the technician started on James. Shortest hair to longest, we figured. James's treatment took about two hours. Once he was combed through, oiled up, and sent to bed with a clear, plastic shower cap on, the technician turned to Julia. It was well past midnight when she finished. If she combed through my hair, we knew we'd be up all night, even though the technician was game to keep going (I believe we were paying a bumped-up hourly rate due to the after-hours nature of her visit). So I had her do a quick run on Michael, paid her almost $800, calculated all the other things I would have loved to spend that money on, and went to sleep.

The next morning the kids went to school, stopping first at the school nurse for the green light to head back to the classroom. I went across town to Lice Enders, thinking I could get a quick appointment and be out in time to pick up the kids and head to the airport. But the place was packed, and even after calling other locations, the earliest I could get in was 3 p.m.

"I might not even have them, but I can't really go on this trip without knowing," I complained to my friend Patricia on the phone. Patricia had four kids and had been through more bouts of lice than probably anyone in the city. I'd called to see if she knew a secret lice-removal source I wasn't aware of.

"Come over here. I can do it," she said.

"What? No, don't be crazy. I can't ask you to do that."

"What other choice do you have?"

When I showed up at Patricia's apartment, she answered the door holding a bag full of lice combs, sprays, and hair clips.

"My sister-in-law in Texas used to own a lice-removal place. I've got her on speakerphone," she said.

I sat down on the toilet in Patricia's bathroom, which got the best natural light in the apartment. She propped her phone on the windowsill and began to section off my hair. For almost two hours, she patiently combed through every strand, peering down at my scalp, picking off the few eggs she found with the tips of her fingers.

"I can never repay you," I said, feeling simultaneously overwhelmed with gratitude and like a disgusting bag of warts.

"I actually find it sort of satisfying," she said, wiping an egg onto a tissue. "And this is what friends do for each other."

Our family went to the mountains. When we arrived, the entire house smelled like tea tree oil. The three blessed (and justifiably paranoid) mothers, Murff, Laura, and Blair, were spraying and squirting it on scalps, hairbrushes, pillows, and T-shirts as a hopeful, preventative measure. Everything I ate that weekend had a faint medicinal taste, but no one else got lice.

———

Sometime in the early aughts, when Michael and I were still dating, we spent an evening playing Trivial Pursuit with a bunch of friends.

Over the course of our relationship, we have played countless board games, most of them in the past decade, since we have had children. Those games I have wiped from my mental hard drive. I try to forget I'm playing Ticket to Ride Europe while I'm still playing Ticket to Ride Europe, honestly. But there are two board game showdowns I remember vividly. One was a game of Pictionary at a motel on Cape Cod—again, when we were young, dating, and had more energy to fight—that ended with Michael walking straight into the Atlantic Ocean after midnight to get away from me, because I would not stop arguing with him about the ineffectiveness of his last drawing. The other was this game of Trivial Pursuit. We only needed one pie piece to win, but so did our friend Vivek, and he landed on the missing color first. One of us pulled out a card. The question asked for the title of Hillary Clinton's 1995 book about society's shared responsibility for caring for children. The room went silent while Vivek thought. I had no idea what the answer was. Hillary Clinton, at that point, was best known for being married to Bill, not as a senator from New York or the secretary of state or a presidential nominee. My feelings about her were neutral to negative, given the fact that I'd grown up in a very Republican home that did not care for her husband. After a minute or two, Vivek's eyes widened. He stood up, pointed a finger in the air, and said, "*It Takes a Village.*" Then, gloating over his victory, he proceeded to run circles around the entire house, screaming, "It Takes a Village! It Takes a Village! It Takes a Village!"

I've never forgotten that night—I *hate* losing Trivial Pursuit—or the name of that book. And now that I have children, I, like every parent in moments of chaos and scheduling hell, say the phrase often. In my mind, it's Vivek's voice, though, echoing through the house as he ran victory laps. "It takes a village!"

Of course, Hillary didn't invent the phrase. It's an old African proverb: "It takes a village to raise a child." Before the proverb, though, there was 1 Corinthians chapter 12, which contains the verses in the Bible about the body of Christ. They aren't referencing children specifically; they are really emphasizing the idea that all of us have a part to play, regardless of our differences or how important society deems us to be. The African proverb and Hillary Clinton and 1 Corinthians 12 are all saying the same thing, though—that we need each other, and we aren't meant to do life or marriage or parenting alone. We're called to do it with people we don't have much in common with or even like. "Whether Jews or Gentiles, slave or free," the Bible says (v. 13).

The second part of the chapter talks about how we all have different roles. Some of us are feet. Some are hands. Some are eyes. Some are ears. God has given us each a job, and the body cannot function without all of us working together. We are all important. "If the whole body were an eye, where would the sense of hearing be? If the whole body were an ear, where would the sense of smell be?" (v. 17). This is where I picture Mike Wazowski from *Monsters, Inc.*, who is 80 percent eyeball, walking around. Or a detached Mr. Potato Head ear trying to inch its way down the stairs of its house. The best part of the chapter comes a little later, though, in verses 21 through 27.

> The eye cannot say to the hand, "I don't need you!" And the head cannot say to the feet, "I don't need you!" On the contrary, those parts of the body that seem to be weaker are indispensable, and the parts that we think are less honorable we treat with special honor. And the parts that are unpresentable are treated with special modesty, while our presentable

parts need no special treatment. But God has put the body together, giving greater honor to the parts that lacked it, so that there should be no division in the body, but that its parts should have equal concern for each other. If one part suffers, every part suffers with it; if one part is honored, every part rejoices with it. Now you are the body of Christ, and each one of you is a part of it.

There are so many lessons in those few sentences—how the strong should mourn when the weak are in pain; how we should be lifting up those of us who are overlooked; how we should turn our expectations of power upside-down. Endless implications for society. But I am always struck by the first sentence in verse 21: "The eye cannot say to the hand, 'I don't need you!' And the head cannot say to the feet, 'I don't need you!'"

If you are a working parent in this world, you feel this. There is no way for me to live my life without a village of sorts. I pay sitters. I take up the offers of generous aunts and grandparents. I sign my children up for free, universal pre-K and city-run after-school programs. I think I'm doing what Hillary would tell me to. I am not, however, doing a great job as a member of the body of Christ. That one is harder. Living in community means laying down your life, your time, your money, and your self-sufficiency. And ugh, I am just the absolute worst at that. I have spent much of my adult life saying, "I don't need you."

I'm not sure what part of the body I am (it's a toss-up between mouth and rear end, probably), but I tried for years to live apart from community. All I wanted was to be an independent little pancreas or elbow who could live her life how she wanted, without help or demands from other people. I did not want to need or be needed.

When a friend invited me to a moms' group or a community group or even a book club, I would joke that I'm allergic to community. I'm ashamed to say that my greatest fear was that someone would demand more of me than I was willing to give, emotionally or logistically.

Obviously, this mindset has failed spectacularly.

I joined that moms' group—extremely reluctantly!—when Julia was born, and stayed in it for almost ten years. If I can stay on the body-part train for a moment more, we were a concentrated gathering of tear ducts and leaky nipples. All of our unpresentables were exposed. Experiencing that broken body of women suffering together and shoring each other up changed me. But I had to work at it. We provided meals for about three weeks every time a family had a new baby. I loved making meals because I loved to cook, and other than the one time I presented pork tenderloin and a corn-and-zucchini side dish that had been sautéed with bacon to my friend Johna—who I did not realize was a vegetarian—I was good at it. (We gave that meal to Johna's neighbor, and I ordered them a pizza.)

Cooking and dropping off the meal was easy. Taking the baby out of the mother's arms at the door and sitting down to talk for a few minutes was not. For me, at least. My love language is acts of service, not quality time. "Now if the foot should say, 'Because I am not a hand, I do not belong to the body,' it would not for that reason stop being part of the body. And if the ear should say, 'Because I am not an eye, I do not belong to the body,' it would not for that reason stop being part of the body" (1 Corinthians 12:15–16). My translation: you can try to distance yourself for whatever reason you choose, but you can't really get away. You're attached, like it or not.

Having children primes the pump for being open to community, but you don't have to be a parent. You just have to suffer. And the good news is that we all will—some in small ways, some mightily. There are so many things I love about being in my forties, but one is that most of us who are allergic to neediness have had to completely get over ourselves. The problems are just too deep and widespread. I cannot fix a broken marriage or a child's harrowing diagnosis or a parent's death with a pork tenderloin.[1] I cannot fix it, period. But I've also learned I cannot amputate myself away from the need, as I have done in the past. I'm called to be an ear, an arm, a tear duct.

My mother is in her late seventies. She and her friends have experienced more suffering still. She and many of her best friends are widows. One has lost an adult child. A few have lost their good health or mobility. My mother was my best teacher in how to help while still keeping people at arm's length. She was, and still is, a wizard at doubling recipes and baking casseroles in half-size dishes, so she'll have extras to drop off with a neighbor who just got out of the hospital or a friend with back problems. (This is the winding road of hospitality: we start taking meals when we have babies; we keep going until we have back problems.) She is still not great at letting people do things for her, and I understand, because she raised me to be the same way. "We shall take care of our own messes. We shall not bother others," could have been printed on a sign above our front door.

But I guess the wonder of being in your seventies is that you get over yourself even more than you do in your forties, because my mom is doing a bang-up job as a widowed member of the body

---

1. I will try.

of Christ these days. She doesn't just take meals to her two best friends, both of whom are homebound. She grocery shops for them and takes one to get her hair cut. When her neighbor calls because she ordered too much take-out and has extra, my mother accepts the invitation to go over and eat it. My mother and this woman, who is new to the neighborhood, enjoy each other's company so much and got so tired of having to walk down the street and around the corner to get to each other's front doors that they split the cost of having a gate cut into their shared back fence. It's lovely to watch her need and be needed and be open to both. I hope I continue to get better at it. She's doing great. Really great. Am I going to keep praising my mother for another sentence? I am. I wrote a fairly complimentary chapter about my mother-in-law a few pages back, and I'm no fool.

The miracle of letting yourself need and be needed is that you always get something out of it, either way. Neuroscientists talk about the dopamine and oxytocin hit you get from performing altruistic acts. I call it God's mercy for my inherently selfish character. It is also, in my experience, an antidote to bitterness. When I keep my distance, I am more likely to compare and judge, and bitterness sets in. Communing is the only thing that dissolves it. We have to be in each other's lives in uncomfortable ways to realize that the shiniest among us don't have it all together, and the most annoying are still human.

Those of you who don't subscribe to the body of Christ still know what I'm talking about. That's why Hillary Clinton's book can be a Trivial Pursuit clue. Many of us are paddling hard under the surface trying to be the "presentable parts (that) need no special treatment." I know I am. But then you get lice. And you remember that sometimes you are presentable, and sometimes you are a bile duct. So you sit as still as you can on your friend's toilet and let her be the hands of Jesus. Believe me, it will bless you both.

Chapter 15

WE WALK AWAY

Moving: Part 4

IN THE END, LOIS AND HER DAUGHTER DID NOT HAVE TO GO TO the DMV. Or the post office. The day after we talked to her about the lost ID, Michael remembered something. Our accountant always asked for our driver's licenses to make a copy that he needed to file our tax returns. We knew Lois had an accountant; she talked about him often as a loyal man who had worked for her husband for years. I called and told Lois to ask her accountant if he might have a copy of her license. Turns out, he did, and he mailed it to her that week.

I sent Lois a Christmas card with a photo of our family on the front. *I thought you might want to see what we looked like!* I wrote on the back. *Sending you lots of love. Hope we can meet soon.* A few weeks later, in January, we got an envelope in the mail from Lois.

Inside were two cards. The first was a Christmas card with a watercolor of Bethlehem on the front and a Bible verse. As I opened the card, another piece of paper fell out onto the floor. It was the size of a postcard, with two chipmunks side by side in purple ballet tutus. On the back, Lois wrote, *Elizabeth! You are tu tu awesome! Thank you for helping me. Love, Lois.*

All of my grandparents are dead and have been for some time. All of Michael's grandparents are dead and have been for some time. We didn't have a single grandparent at our wedding in 2005. I was starting to feel about Lois the way I remembered feeling about my grandparents (even though, at eighty-one, Lois was really the same age as our mothers). There was no parent-child baggage to weigh us down. She was easy to please and always happy to hear my voice. I half expected a ten-dollar bill or a stick of gum to fall out of that card. If Lois had email, she did not tell us, and on the rare occasion she did not pick up her phone, a recording told me that her voice mailbox was not active. As was the case with both of my grandmothers, we had to talk on the phone until Lois felt like hanging up. Every once in a while there would be a pause long enough for me to explain that I'd arrived at home/work/school pickup and had to go, but otherwise, I stayed on the line, mostly listening.

In mid-January, the president of our old building's co-op board, who still occasionally checked in with Michael, texted to let him know that Lois's title transfer was approved and finalized. The apartment was in her name. We could all sign the contract.

Lois's lawyer, Paul, emailed back the contract we had sent to him six months earlier. All we had to do was sign and wire a deposit, he wrote. I was writing at the library, not checking email, when Michael texted me.

Paul sent back the contract. Price is increased $500K. And
he has us paying the flip tax and transfer taxes.

Reading that the lawyer increased the price by half a million
dollars brings up the obvious point—we were already offering
more than half a million dollars for a two-thousand-square-foot
apartment that was uninhabitable in its peeling plaster, hoarder-
level, water-damaged state. Kind of a lot more. (If I told you
exactly how much we offered, all of the blood vessels in your
eyeballs would burst at once, unless you live in New York, in
which case you'd think it was a steal.) The flip tax, should you be
curious, is a 2 percent tax paid by a seller that goes into the coffers
of the co-op. Flip taxes are how the building keeps its finances
flush. It isn't unheard of for a seller to ask the buyer to take on
that expense, especially if the buyer is eager. But to increase the
purchase price by $500,000 without any sort of conversation was
madness. We could not figure out Paul's angle. He wasn't Lois's
real estate agent. Why would he care how much the apartment
sold for? His fee certainly didn't change with the price on the contract. Michael had mentioned a few times that Paul seemed cagey
on the phone and unresponsive over email. Our lawyer could
never get him to return a call. I always gave him the benefit of the
doubt, knowing that Lois was a unique individual and probably
not his highest priority.

"Maybe this is just his way of haggling, of trying to be a good
advocate and get her the best price possible," I said.

"But this isn't how you do it. You don't sit on a contract for six
months and then, with no explanation, counter with that big of a
jump," Michael said. "Oh, and in his email, he also said that you
should stop contacting Lois and only communicate with him."

Hmm. That part was weird.

We assumed that Paul had discussed the counteroffer with Lois, although it seemed strange that she had never indicated that she was unhappy with the original amount we'd offered. In fact, she'd said multiple times to me that she didn't care about the money, she just wanted it settled. (I mean, I never truly believed that, but the point is, she didn't strike me as a ruthless negotiator.) When Michael called Paul to try to understand where that exorbitantly high number came from, he would not give a straight answer. He kept saying, "My client asked that your wife not call her anymore."

"Really?" Michael said. "That's surprising to me, considering she just mailed my wife a Christmas card."

Michael and I decided that I wouldn't call Lois back right away. We were always willing to go up a bit, but we didn't want to waste a lot of time going back and forth. We'd talk to our bank and get the final, get-a-grip, don't-push-it number they were comfortable with us offering, given the added cost of the construction loan, and then email Paul back with that amount and say take it or leave it. Which we did.

"And what do we do if she doesn't take it?" I asked him.

"We walk away," he said.

"Eh, but do we?"

This was the problem. We had no leverage. Forget the fact that we were so emotionally invested in getting this apartment and moving back into our building that every acquaintance, from our closest friends to casual coworkers, asked us, "So, what's up with that apartment?" every time we saw them. (We had to stop talking about it constantly, but how? It's all we thought about.) We looked at StreetEasy daily, and there were not any apartments we could afford that came close to the size of Lois's in our neighborhood or the surrounding ones. It was that simple. The deal was too good to let go of.

"We cannot afford anything close to what he's asking for, so yes. If the price doesn't come down, we have to walk away," Michael said, softly, looking intently at me.

"Ugh, you're right. I know. I guess that would make it easy. But what did we miss? How could she ask for this much with no warning?"

Once we made our final offer, I called Lois to, ostensibly, fill her in. But I was fishing around to see if I could gauge whether she was the one telling Paul to increase the price, while playing footsie with me. Surely we hadn't completely misread her. Correction: Surely I hadn't completely misread her. There was a very thin wisp of accusation that I, being the only one who had talked to Lois in the past eight months, had convinced myself we were friends and missed a clue that she was a cunning business-woman. Had I? Was it possible that all this time, I had been bending over backward to make it clear that we were not trying to take advantage of an old lady, and the old lady actually had my number?

But when Lois picked up, she was warm and upbeat, as usual. I thanked her for the Christmas card and then explained where we were. When I said her lawyer had upped the price significantly, and I assumed she was aware, she cut me off.

"No. No, no, no, no, I was not aware. He did *what*?" Lois told me she was using a new phone. The sound kept fading in and out. It was as if she had put the phone on speaker but then hid it under a pile of laundry.

I asked if she knew that Paul told us that she didn't want me calling her anymore. There was rustling and mumbling that I couldn't decipher. I could hear her getting louder and more worked up, but nothing came through clearly.

"Lois? Lois! I can't hear you."

"Okay, is that better?" She readjusted the phone. "Are you telling me that this man is trying to come between you and me? NO."

"Well, that's good to hear . . ."

"And when he calls me back, I am telling him to take your offer!"

I got off the phone feeling confident that we had righted a wrong. I was reassured that Lois was telling me the truth, that Paul was the enemy, and that she had gotten through to him. Then a week passed. Two. We emailed Paul. Our lawyer emailed Paul. I cannot express to you how exasperating it was to consistently email this guy and never hear back. Finally, Michael called his office. Paul doubled down on his story, claiming that Lois really didn't care about selling the apartment, that she would hold out for more money, and that she absolutely did not want me contacting her. "She'll take fifty thousand dollars off of her price," he finally conceded. We felt like we were in the Twilight Zone.

One of two things was happening. Either Paul was lying, or Lois was playing both sides, and every conversation we'd had was some sort of game, at best, or outright deception, at worst. Lois called me back and emphatically told me that she called Paul and told him to take our offer. A few days later, we got another contract. The price hadn't budged.

"I feel insane," I said to Michael in bed one night. "Are we idiots? Have we been had?"

"Maybe. Maybe Lois is playing innocent with you and telling Paul to go for the kill. Maybe she's crazy like a fox," he said.

"But why go through the tortuous process of getting the title transfer?"

"I don't know. None of it makes sense."

"I don't think she's playing us."

"I don't know anything anymore."

"I just want it to end. Yes or no. How do we make this end?"

"We walk away. That's how it ends."

"But I don't want to walk away. I think this is our forever home."

"I don't want to, either."

I called Lois one last time. I told her that, once again, Paul had sent back the contract with the higher price on it. I asked if she told him to do that. It was okay if you did, I told her. I just wanted to know the truth so that we could move on. We could not pay the higher price. We did not think the apartment was worth that much. We really wanted to buy it, I said, we really did. I was so grateful to have gotten to know you, I said. But this was it.

Lois had gone to the Verizon store to get a different phone, after the last one made it hard to hear her. Now she was loud and clear. And, I could tell, furious. She insisted that Paul was lying, and she would fix it. She said she'd call him and then call me back that night. I went to bed, having never heard from her.

Every day was a circle. We would think we were making progress, that we had a grip on reality and Lois's intentions, and then by the end of the day, we'd be back at the bottom, wondering what was real. Maybe we'd be better off buying another apartment after all—something smaller, yes, but with fewer negotiations in which it felt like everyone was using a Magic 8 Ball to make decisions. I thought about our obligation to Lois. If—big if!—she was being honest with us, if Paul was misrepresenting her, and we backed out, she also lost. Was it crossing a line to find her a new lawyer? Was that compassionate? Or a conflict of interest?

I woke up in the morning and prayed. Again. Open hands, I told myself. "God," I said. "We are tired. We are confused. Show us the next step to take. If it's a yes or a no, we will go where you tell us to go. Resolve this, please. Give us the ending."

An hour later Paul emailed us a contract with the price we offered and all of the taxes resolved.

That afternoon, Lois called me. I was excited to tell her the good news, but she sounded distraught.

"I called you! I've been calling you! Oh, I'm so glad I got you. I thought you'd blocked me," she said.

"What are you talking about?"

"I have this new phone! I wrote down your number the other day, when you told me, but I wrote one number wrong. I was calling and calling last night, and the number said it was blocked. I thought I'd lost you. I thought you didn't want to talk to me, that that lawyer had done something bad. And then I listened to a message you left me on my answering machine, thank goodness, and I got your right number! Did he send it? Did he send the contract?"

"Yes, Lois. He sent the right contract. We are all set. We're going to sign it today."

"I told him that he worked for *me*. And I told him that if you walked away from this deal, I was reporting him to the bar association."

"Well, whatever you said worked."

"And after this, I'm getting a new lawyer."

We talked for about half an hour, until I told her I needed to make dinner.

"Okay, yes, you go. But listen, my husband would be so happy. He was a good man, a good man. He was so good-looking, so handsome. No one could ever say a bad word about him. He was an angel, you know."

"Yes, Lois. I know."

Chapter 16

FUNERALS ARE THE NEW GIRLS' TRIPS

THERE WAS ONCE A YEAR WHEN MICHAEL AND I WERE INVITED
to fourteen weddings. We attended twelve. That year almost bankrupted us. The only reason that the festivities haven't run together in one stressful blur—other than that these were weddings of people we adored, and for whom we were giddy and hopeful—is that I was pregnant with Julia during most of them, and therefore I was sober as a judge. Actually, I got pregnant with Julia at one of the first of the twelve weddings, an affair in Florida where, right before the ceremony, I stabbed my abdomen with a syringe full of drugs to make me ovulate and conceived my daughter sometime around 5 a.m.

With apologies to two of the couples who were kind enough to invite us to witness their marriages that year, I actually have forgotten whose weddings we skipped. But the rest were un-skippable: college roommates, cousins, our dearest childhood friends. They just all happened to wed from the fall of 2008 to the tail end of 2009. Two of my best friends, Catherine and Hallie, got married while I was still hiding my pregnancy. At their receptions I would dance for a song, then have to sit down and eat a piece of bread to avoid wanting to vomit, while Michael would sip from his own glass and also whatever drink someone insisted I have, covering for me and widening the gap between our states of sobriety. In September 2009 we attended a wedding on Cape Cod, where I was, obviously, the designated driver back to the hotel from the reception. At the time, Michael and I owned a Mercury Sable that was in such bad shape, its power steering had failed. To make a left turn, you had to pull hand over hand as if you were a valiant captain in a Disney movie, trying to right a ship during a hurricane, just to get the steering wheel to move. Mind you, I was already adding a level of difficulty by tucking a pregnant torso behind the wheel, so I flatly refused to put forth the effort to make left turns. It took me half an hour just to get out of the parking lot.

We flew to San Francisco and Winston-Salem and Chattanooga. One wedding was in rural Wyoming, requiring us to fly to Denver and drive a few hours. For that flight, we arrived late at JFK airport because of standstill traffic, and when we tried to check our bag, the gate agent told us it was less than an hour before our flight and rules dictated that we were not allowed to. My mother-in-law had driven us to the airport, so Michael called her to circle back around. The thing about my mother-in-law is that her car is a bit like the Cat in the Hat's Thingamajigger—belching smoke from one side and full of unexpected tools. My mother-in-law is known for having at least twenty-seven tote bags on her person at any given moment. We decided to each grab two large totes from the floorboards of the back seat, stuff in the items we couldn't do without—a cocktail dress I'd borrowed from a friend that would fit my six-month pregnant belly, for example—and leave everything else behind. On the sidewalk outside departures, Michael and I unzipped our large duffel and shoved whatever we could into carry-on totes. I ran back into the terminal carrying a faux Goyard bag my mother-in-law bought on Canal Street, maternity bras hanging out the side. Once we finally arrived in Wyoming, we filled in with socks, T-shirts, sweatpants, and toiletries from the local Dollar General.

My cousin Sam's wedding in the Hudson Valley was the last one of the year. By then we had maxed out our credit card and were barely able to pay our mortgage. My parents came to that wedding. I believe they bought an extra gift and put my name on it.

This is the truth: if I could go back, the only thing I would change is going to the two weddings we missed. A few years later we were invited to my friend Olivia's wedding in Greece. We didn't go, because—this sounds like a joke and is the god's honest truth— we'd already flown to a wedding in Greece, my friend Eleni's, two months before. I don't know what to say. We have several close acquaintances with ties to Greece. But every time I think about Olivia's wedding or see a photo of her standing in the moonlight on the island of Hydra with the puffed sleeves of her dress around her face, I regret missing it. Being able to say, "I was at your wedding," is reapplying adhesive to all the old friendships that have slid away.

I'm not in the business of giving advice, only telling you the ways I've messed up to offer some warning. But if you are reading this and you are younger than I am, a full schedule of life events ahead of you, I want to tell you this: go to the weddings. Every one you possibly can. And when the time comes, go to the funerals. If it almost bankrupts you, go.

When you grow up where I grew up and go to college where I went to college, a lot of your friends get married in their twenties.

Not all, but many. Summers would roll around in the years after we graduated, and we would spend a weekend in our hometowns or at someone's parents' beach house, packing taffeta bridesmaid dresses carefully in hanging bags. We would get on stage to dance to "Mustang Sally" and "Proud Mary" and end the night in the Krystal's or Bojangle's drive-through. A month or two later, we'd do it all again. New boyfriends or husbands would filter in, and weddings were an ideal way to scope them out. Did they add to or take away from our friends? Were they insistent that their girlfriend or wife stay with them, seated at a table? Or did they ask the bride's grandmother to dance? We liked the guys who danced with the grandmothers the most.

There arrives a time when the weddings peter out. For me, that time was shortly after the Year of a Dozen Weddings. We had a couple of stragglers in 2010 and 2011, and then one of Michael's college roommates got married on Mackinac Island, Michigan, in 2012, when James was five weeks old. Another friend, Caitie, had a newborn four days younger, and we sat in the back of the rehearsal dinner with our dresses pulled down to our waistlines, exhausted and breastfeeding those two boys on a banquette over-looking the World's Longest Porch (TM) at the Grand Hotel. On the drive back to the airport, the only thing that kept James from screaming was sucking on my pinky that had been dipped in Diet Dr Pepper. Even so, I love that we went. I saw Caitie last summer. Those boys were now ten. We laughed about calling the hotel to ask about babysitters for the wedding ceremony, and the front desk told us, "Call housekeeping. Same thing." We looked at each other. *Same thing?* But we did. And two women from the housekeeping staff knocked on our doors in the late afternoon, took our babies, and rocked and cuddled them while we watched our husbands be groomsmen and drank cocktails and pumped milk and poured it down the bathroom sink. I know I was tired and cranky most of that weekend. When I think about it now, though, enough time has passed that the whole trip, the beauty and the absurd, is net positive.

While you are still in the throes of weddings, even as the celebrations become further and further apart, you take for granted that you will see your friends a few times a year. Maybe you have had a baby, so you lose large blocks of time—months, years—wasting all of your brain cells trying to get every human in your household to sleep contiguously for at least six hours. At the same time, you and your friends are going to graduate school, moving cities, and changing jobs. It takes a while to realize that you don't see your old friends as much as you used to. This is when you start planning girls' trips.

I wish we could call them women's trips, because we are grown women, but I can't. They are girls' trips. Someone already decided.

My four best friends from childhood and I try to take a girls' trip every February. These trips can be difficult to plan and threaten to fall apart multiple times, but they are never financially straining, as weddings once were, because we are all pretty cheap. Murff would always pay more for the trip than the rest of us, but only because February directly follows January, which is duck season in hunting circles, and her husband hunts. By the time February rolls around, she has calculated the time her husband spent duck hunting in vacation dollars, and it adds up to, roughly, a month in Paris. I'm right behind Murff in terms of wanting something fancy, because I keep track of how many hours my husband plays golf. Fortunately Hallie, Vanessa, and Blair are more mature. And cost-conscious.

For several years we stayed for free at a house in Florida that Murff's parents rented for the winter. The downstairs level had its own entrance and kitchenette, but Murff's parents were upstairs for the whole trip, shouting down a few times a day to ask if we were alright or anyone wanted coffee cake. One year Blair was in the hospital, on bed rest with a pregnancy complication, so we all flew to Memphis and sat in her room eating burritos for two days. In the summer of 2021, after postponing our trip for a year and a half, we spent twenty-four hours in Mound City, Arkansas, just over the Mississippi River from Memphis, in a cottage owned by Blair's aunt and uncle. We had to move fast, taking turns unzipping our souls as efficiently as possible so that we could properly catch up and still deal with everyone's anxieties and marital problems and general crap before it was time to go home. We managed.

The girls' trips keep us close—closer, even, than we were as kids, despite the fact that we spent hours upon hours in each other's houses and pools and sleeping bags as kids and now see each other once or twice a year at most. At every stage of life, I think, we need each other more, because life gets infinitely harder. We only *thought* we were suffering in high school. Now we have real problems.

In the past three or so years we have entered a new stage in which we travel for funerals. Our parents have started dying. It's awful. But these days, this is sometimes how friends reconnect: not at girls' trips, but at funerals. It's the groundwork of the girls' trips that makes buying the last-minute plane ticket without blinking, without a second of hesitation, easy. When my dad died, Vanessa flew from Tucson, where she now lives, even though the funeral was right before New Year's—a terrible time to book a flight. Hallie drove up from Birmingham. Murff and Blair live in Memphis, so they didn't have to travel, but they kept my children and organized food deliveries and deposited coolers of fried chicken and smoked salmon in my mother's kitchen. Hallie's dad died a year and a half before mine. Sam was two weeks old. My parents, who also loved Hallie's dad, were still in New York City, helping us through the newborn days, instead of at home in Memphis, where the funeral was. "You need to go," they said. "We will stay here with the other kids." And so I did. Sam was a less-than-robust breastfeeder and had lost weight in his second week of life. The day before we left, our pediatrician put us on a schedule of pumping and formula supplementing that was causing a lot of frustration (me) and vomit (him). Still, the two of us boarded a plane.

I've flown to three more funerals since that one. My own dad's. My dad's cousin Marvin's funeral, which was in Dallas. I am close to Marvin's kids, two of whom lived in New York at the time, and I felt like someone from our family needed to be there. And then there was my friend Amy's mom, Susie. Susie, who gave me life-changing advice about mothers-in-law when I was a newlywed. I flew to South Carolina for Susie's funeral. No one would have blamed me if I didn't show up to Dallas or Greenville. You don't get an advance invitation to funerals. They are usually inconvenient and expensive. But I remember all of the unexpected people who showed up to my dad's funeral. My cousins, who lived out of town. Catherine, who flew in from DC. Merritt, who drove from Nashville to Memphis, got out of her car, hugged me for fifteen seconds in the hallway of the funeral home, got directly back into her car, and drove home. When I think about that, I laugh and tear up. It was ridiculous and a beautiful act of friendship. So I implore you, go to the funerals.

Plus, if I can be crass for a split second, traveling alone to a funeral can be great, especially if you are a parent. For Susie's funeral I flew alone and slept in a dark hotel room, which was magnificent. At Marvin's funeral I stayed an extra day, turned the weekend into a mini writing retreat, and ate Tex-Mex from the mall across the street. Also paradise.

Life is cyclical, and at some point in the not-too-distant future, I'll be invited to my friends' children's weddings. Ostensibly my own children might have weddings, but I'm not prepared to think about that yet. When that season comes, it will be glorious. I will buy better gifts. Until then I will purchase plane tickets for girls' trips and funerals, and I will eat good food and cry, surrounded by those who love me—and I, them—unconditionally. And it will be worth it, every single time.

Chapter 17

STAYING PUT

I AM NOT THE BEST PERSON TO ASK ABOUT WHAT IT WAS LIKE living in New York City during the earliest days of the pandemic. I lie. Or, I should say, I lied. A little, when asked. I happened to be promoting my first book in the winter of 2021, when the previous spring was still fresh on everyone's minds, and each podcast host and book club reader I talked to wanted to know the same thing. How was it during those first few months? Did everyone leave? Did we?

We stayed. That was the truth. But I was relentlessly upbeat about our circumstances, which, in hindsight, was a teensy bit of a show.

After 9/11, which I also lived through in New York, the rest of the country showered us with love. The city had been attacked, and the world wrapped its arms around our little island. Tourists returned and bought tickets to Broadway shows and ate in our restaurants and poured money into our economy. In a bout of hysterical blindness, everyone loved Rudy Giuliani, remember? I'm not comparing the experiences of 9/11 and the pandemic; they were completely different animals with a different set of solutions. But it's just to say that when Covid hit New York, before we knew much about it, when the virus hadn't affected the rest of the country in the same way, there was a sense that New York City, in its essence, was culpable. I sensed disdain from people inside and outside the gates. Look at us, riding crowded subways and packing into tiny bars and living on top of each other in our overpriced apartments. What did we think was going to happen?

So, as one does when one loves a complicated place—which is every place; I'm from the Deep South, I know these things—I got defensive. Judgmental, actually. First I was really mad at people who left. Not the ones who, for example, had a new baby and went to live with their parents to get help with the newborn while they worked from home. Or friends who worked in the theater district and suddenly had no income and couldn't afford their rent. No, I'm talking about the friends who had a lot of money, our rich friends, who decided to use the freedom from commuting and school to rent a house in Utah for ski season. Or friends who got long-term Airbnb homes in the Poconos, even though their apartments in the city were twice the size of mine. I was awful about those people, complaining endlessly to my husband, who began to just nod silently and squeeze my hand while I ranted.

"I heard they can't even get reliable Wi-Fi in that house they rented. I mean, how's that going for work? You know where we have Wi-Fi? Manhattan," I'd say.

"Mmm-hmm." Squeeze.

"Oh, and what about all of the people who could benefit from their money in this city? The guy at the bodega where they'd normally be getting a sandwich? The housekeeper! I bet they aren't still paying their housekeeper. What about their tax dollars? We sure could use those tax dollars right now!"

"Babe, they are still paying income tax in New York City."

"ARE THEY?"

"Yes. Yes, they are. I hear you on the bodega guy, though."

I was seething, like someone had injured my child, and I was on a hunt for my pound of flesh. I tried to lure other people into my rage bubble. "Can you believe?" I'd start. "Utah? What, they can just RENT a HOUSE in UTAH?" And when any friend extended graciousness or sympathy, an iota of understanding that maybe we were all navigating this scary time differently, or maybe this family had other things going on that necessitated a change of scenery, I started complaining about that friend too. When Andrew Yang was early in his candidacy for mayor in 2020, he gave an interview to the *New York Times* in which he defended leaving Manhattan for his family's country home upstate. He said, "Can you imagine trying to have two kids on virtual school in a two-bedroom apartment, and then trying to do work yourself?" Predictably, I wasn't the only parent who lost her kettle chips over that one.

When a comedy club owner wrote an op-ed declaring that New York City was over—and he'd be living out the rest of his days in Miami—Jerry Seinfeld, patron saint of the Upper West Side, wrote a counter op-ed in the *Times* calling that guy out. I practically memorized it. Seinfeld wrote:

> He says he knows people who have left New York for Maine, Vermont, Tennessee, Indiana. I have been to all of these places many, many, many times over many decades. And with all due respect and affection, Are . . . You . . . Kidding . . . Me?

A construction site next door to the New York Society Library blew up Seinfeld's op-ed and made it into a huge banner that hung down about six stories on the outside of the new building that was rising over Madison Avenue. It was the kind of over-the-top waste of money you see all over New York City, which I love and hate with equal measure. The banner brought me a lot of joy when I began commuting back to the library for work, even though Seinfeld was being snippy and low-key making fun of my home state. I realized in those early months that my reaction wasn't the result of being scared New York was dead forever. (I never really believed that.) It was that even if New York didn't recover, even if it staggered as a shell of its former self, dull and dirty (which did happen, although not for nearly as long as everyone predicted), I was still devoted to it. And what made me so angry was that, in my opinion, people were leaving because it wasn't serving them. It wasn't fun. Nothing was open. It wasn't exciting. There were months, before take-out resumed en masse, when you had to cook! That was a deal breaker in ways you can't imagine for some New Yorkers. I wanted people to love the city at her worst, like I did, and I felt they didn't, and I was ticked off.

So when anyone asked how things were going, I was determined to paint an optimistic picture. Yes, there was a field hospital of white tents springing up like ominous mushrooms on a grassy field in Central Park that my kids could see as they climbed trees near our house. Yes, I felt like the walls were closing in on me. We had no home office or backyard. Michael worked from a corner of our bedroom. I stopped working entirely. He did an army-sized grocery shop once every two weeks at midnight or 1 a.m. to avoid the crowds, coming home with more meat than we could fit in the freezer and produce that would go bad before we'd eat it all. We fought. He wanted appreciation for doing the work. I wanted fewer packs of chicken thighs. But I glossed over those things in conversation, focusing instead on the moments of grace and service and community I was seeing all around me.

And I wasn't inventing those moments. Living on top of each other had its benefits. Our building has dozens of elderly people who live alone, and our proximity allowed us not just to grocery shop for them but carry a portion of our dinner down in the elevator every few nights. Lockdown never felt isolating for us, because we had neighbors in our lobby waving to us from across the hallway, taking turns using the elevators. We learned that the family next door, who had a toddler a few months older than Sam, liked to fly kites in the fields in Central Park closest to our house, so we would meet them at the same time most days, and the boys played. Small interactions, even from a distance, were filled with deep connection and care. In all my years in New York City, I think I felt the least alone.

So I apologize if you talked to me in 2020 and I made it seem like life was grand here in New York City. It was. And it was also awful. It's better now. Most of our friends who left came back. Some stayed away permanently. Jerry Seinfeld definitely wrote that op-ed from his house in the Hamptons. No one is perfect.

My mother has a saying for when it's raining but the sun is poking through the clouds. Others might call it a sunshower. In my mother's Mississippi diction, however, this particular weather event is "the devil beating his wife." Who knows why. Maybe the devil's wife is a nice supernatural being? The sunshine? And the rain is his anger lashing out? I didn't even know Satan was married. But it's a reminder to me that, most often in my life, the desperate times reveal the most goodness. Not necessarily growth out of hardship in my own heart, although that's a great goal, too, but more that weakness and times of brokenness point me to other people who come alongside me and help carry the burden.

During the fall of 2020, the helpers were two women who lived in my building. My two oldest kids started school that semester on a hybrid schedule, so they were in the school building two to three days a week and home the rest. After a disastrous spring, I knew we needed to figure out a way for them to have a separate space from the rest of the family for logging on to remote school. Our rotating cast of part-time sitters had started coming back to our apartment to help care for Sam, which only added another adult human being to our already crowded space on a daily basis. We were still crawling out from under the togetherness, licking our wounds.

I knew the family that lived in the apartment directly below us had temporarily relocated. I asked if we could possibly use their place for remote school. Of course, Delia, the mother, texted me within minutes. Whatever you need. And she sent me the code to the lockbox in the lobby where they stored a spare key. From then on, a few mornings a week, Julia and James packed their backpacks as if they were going to school, walked down a flight of stairs, and sat at our neighbor's dining room table, where it was quiet, to do school. Everything was going swimmingly until another neighbor in the building, Nikki, had a toilet pipe burst in the apartment above hers, causing extensive damage that was going to require renovating much of her kitchen. Nikki sent an email to our co-op's listserv, asking if anyone was gone and if she could sublet their apartment for a few months. Delia texted me.

I'm talking to Nikki about letting her use our place. But let me
know what hours you'll need to be there so we can work out
the details.

I texted back.

Don't worry about us! We'll just do school from our place.
Nikki needs yours more than we do. We'll be fine.

No, I already told Nikki that the Passarella kids come as part
of the package.

And thus began a months-long arrangement where, one or two
days a week, we used a neighbor's apartment that was also being
used by another neighbor. I would text Nikki around 8:15 a.m. to
let her know we were finishing breakfast and heading down, and
Nikki—whose job was still remote; she had no office she needed
to go to—would clear out, to who knows where, until school was
finished at 2:30. My kids sat through meetings and did their work
while playing with Nikki's cats, and I did as much work as I could
at Delia's/Nikki's desk in the bedroom, in between uploading reading journal entries and printing math worksheets. One day we left
a loaf of banana bread and a thank-you note for Nikki on our way
out. That night I got a text from her.

It was so kind of you to make banana bread for me. It
happens to be high on my list of comfort foods. I am
genuinely happy to be able to share Delia's apartment. It
makes me feel like I'm making some small contribution to
getting us through this experience.

The next week Nikki left homemade haystack cookies for the kids.

"This is why people are attracted to living in communes," I said that night to Michael.

Having Delia's apartment to spread out in, having Nikki acknowledge that we were all in this together, those were the small acts that got me through the worst days. Months later I was able to see that I couldn't talk about the goodness of my neighbors and the resilience of my community unless I acknowledged why they showed up in the first place, why the cheering for health-care workers out of the windows at 7 p.m. felt so healing, why I needed to beat the drum of positivity about New York City to anyone who would listen—because I was falling apart. I mean, we all were. But some of us have a much harder time admitting it. I am those some of us.

——————

My older children are big fans of writer and native Floridian Carl Hiaasen's young reader books, which are named *Flush* and *Squirm* and *Chomp* after the creatures of the swampy Florida ecosystem that show up in the stories. A couple of years ago, I read *Hoot* aloud to the two of them at bedtime over the course of a few weeks. The crux of the plot of *Hoot* involves a flock of burrowing owls whose nests are about to be destroyed by a pancake chain hoping to build a new restaurant on the empty lot. Burrowing owls are adorable. They have long legs that look like pipe cleaners and have been called "howdy birds" for the way they pop their heads out of their tunnels and nod. In the western part of the United States, burrowing owls move into vacant tunnels left by prairie dogs or armadillos. In Florida, where Hiaasen's burrowing owls were, they dig their own. They've been known to line the entrance with animal dung to attract bugs that then provide an easy meal.

I often feel like a burrowing owl. I'm friendly and extroverted. I'm the howdiest of howdy birds. I will howdy until I'm blue in the face, because I like to project an aura of competence and fun (!) or at least distract you from whatever gong show is circling my lower legs in the form of my four-year-old. It makes perfect sense to me, however, that these howdy birds are insistent on digging their own holes. I do that too. I can be stubbornly set in my ways about things. Some of those have served me well. I know what I like in terms of clothing and home decor. I wear the same rotation of jeans and shirts in shades of black, navy, and grey every day, and I've painted multiple foyers in different apartments the exact same shade of brown (a Benjamin Moore shade that is now *discontinued*, and I'm not over it).

Other holes aren't great. I feel attacked when dental hygienists subtly shame me for not buying the correct brand of electric toothbrush or flossing enough, and I become morally indignant about it. Therefore I avoid going to the dentist until I can feel my teeth jangling in their rotted roots as I walk in hard shoes on a frozen sidewalk. Last month I had a sinus infection so painful and resistant to at-home remedies that had worked in the past that I looked up if cavities could be bad enough to travel upward through your jawbones and infect the insides of your face.

I hate accepting help from people.

I'm really strong, so I don't even need them, anyway.

I'm a better friend, daughter, sister, and wife than mother, and I don't think that will ever change.

I'm angry a lot but anxious almost never, and I tell myself one balances out the other. (It doesn't.)

I think New York City is part of my identity, and I'm meant to live here forever.

Burrowing deep into those truths about myself makes me feel settled and safe. To get out of them, to move even a little in my understanding or opinion, I have to crawl through the dung at the entrance. That's usually how it goes. I've found as I've gotten older that, most of the time, making those moves is worth it. I am embracing being vulnerable with my community here in small doses. I accepted *more than one* meal delivery when my husband was in the hospital *and did not even write thank-you notes*. I've learned how to use my angry temperament to identify with my daughter instead of push her away. Did you know that despite the fact that burrowing owls can fly, they are frequently hit by cars while running across the road? Trying new things can be lifesaving.

I'm still dug in deep on New York City. That is one hole I won't crawl out of. You should know this about me by now; I couldn't even move to a different building. But I have forgiven the people who left. My conclusion is that some people can only begin to piece themselves back together with a change of scenery. They needed to move away. I fell apart and could only begin to feel like myself when the city did as well. I had to be put back together alongside her. I needed to stay.

Epilogue

FINALLY, FINALLY

EVERY TIME I TALKED TO LOIS ON THE PHONE, I IMAGINED WHAT she looked like, in the same way that when you read a book, you're imagining the protagonist as Meryl Streep or Zendaya or, if he's a tenderhearted stallion and you're feeling frisky, obviously Sam Heughan, the guy from *Outlander*. I knew Lois was a Black woman in her eighties with occasional high blood pressure who could not be pushed around. She did not sound like a tall person, which I realize is nuts, but it's just how I felt. Her voice always conjured a woman who had *seen* some *stuff* and yet took loving care of the people around her. I can't explain it, but for some reason, the picture that came to mind more often than not was of Tina Turner. And you know what? I was kind of spot on.

The day before we closed on the apartment—more than fourteen months after I first wrote to her and asked if she might be willing to sell—Lois and I met for the first time. Until we had signed all of the papers and handed over the check, I was nervous she'd change her mind. I also wanted to be clear that we were going to start throwing out the contents of the apartment a few days after the closing. We'd bought it as is, and I knew she knew that. Even so, I told her that if there was anything, anything at all, that she might want, she should come walk through the apartment before we owned it.

"I think there are some hurricane lamps I might want," Lois said.

"Okay, how about ten o'clock on Tuesday morning?" I said.

"Ohhh, yes, ten o'clock. See you then."

She was right on time. I was early. I thought that if I could find the lamps before she arrived, I could have them sitting in the foyer, ready to go, and maybe she wouldn't start picking through other items or second-guessing her decision to sign it all over to us. When I was in high school and my boyfriend, who took his sweet, sweet time before our first kiss, would turn onto my street, I would start shivering. My teeth would chatter. This was—still is—how my body responds to being nervous or anticipating an unknown event. Will he or won't he, when we pull in the driveway? Chills would flutter through my torso until I let the vibrations out like a horse neighing. Attractive! Anyway, I was wandering through the apartment, shaking out my arms at my sides as shudders came and went, waiting on Lois. Part of me (most of me) couldn't wait to meet her. Michael and I were both consumed with her, reading into every move she made for months. I want to say it was like meeting someone you'd been flirting with online, except I've never done that. Showing my age here, but let's say it was like when the host took away the partition at the end of *The Dating Game*, and the contestant got to lay eyes on her bachelor for the first time. So there I was, quivering and thumbing through a bunch of desk calendars from 1984 when I heard the back door open.

Lois came around the corner pulling a two-wheeled grocery cart that appeared to be heavy, by the way she was breathing, although when I looked down at it later, it was filled with other empty totes. "Hellooo!" she said, straightening up and setting the cart against a table. I could barely see her face, as she was wearing a black face mask and a hat pulled low over her eyes, but there was so much more to take in, it didn't matter. Her hair was long and wild, bouncing around her shoulders like Wonder Woman's. She'd accessorized her black straw hat with a glittery silver brooch in the shape of a bow. She had a blue and red silk scarf tied around her neck and was wearing a black jumpsuit with a black leather corset (a corset!) around the middle. On top of the jumpsuit, she had on a long, black duster jacket with a hot pink silk flower the size of a baby's head pinned to the lapel. She was slightly disheveled and fragile and eccentric and luminous. Exactly right. I walked forward and gave her a hug.

"Finally, finally," she said, softly patting my back.

The first order of business for Lois was the keys. Oh, the keys. She thought it would be best to give them to me ahead of the closing, so that we could make sure to find the ones to the mailbox and determine if all of them worked. Out of a bag stuffed down into her cart she pulled out two wads of keys I can only describe as looking like dense bunches of grapes that also got tangled in some garbage at the bottom of the sea. There were dozens, maybe hundreds of keys. I started to ask where on earth the rest of them went, as it appeared she had enough to unlock every storage unit in the Midwest, but I refrained, because I thought we might be there until dinner trying to find ours, and I shouldn't distract her. Soon enough, though, Lois held up a bunch of keys, squinted at one section, unclipped a couple from the wad, and passed them over. They worked.

We set out to find the lamps, which, it turned out, were perched on top of one of the very tall metal cabinets that contained loads and loads of prescription medications (we found the keys to those cabinets, too, miraculously), almost touching the ceiling. To get them down I had to wedge a rolling stool in between a rusted-out air conditioning unit and a box of unopened wrist braces to keep it steady, then inch the lamps over with the tips of my fingers until they started to fall and I caught them. After all that, she took one look, waved a hand over them, and said, "I changed my mind."

"If it's that you are worried about getting them in and out of a cab by yourself, I can drive you home in my car," I told her.

"No, it's not that," she said. "I don't need these. Not any of this."

Lois turned and started walking back to the front of the apartment. She pointed out a few of the furniture items that had been hers ("the pretty ones") and mentioned that the apartment wasn't as cluttered before her husband stopped practicing medicine. After he retired, he began moving things from other houses he owned into the apartment and, she said, ordering stuff online at night. "That's how it got this way," she said. I had been so worried she would succumb to the pull of his memory and not be able, in the end, to let anything go, but I was wrong. I think, in a way, the apartment's haywire state represented someone she didn't recognize, maybe a person her husband became later in life, not whom she fell in love with. She seemed relieved to be done with the whole situation.

In the entry hall was a hutch that had a few knickknacks on its shelves. Lois picked up a ceramic camel. The animal was sitting, its legs tucked under its body, and it was glazed a soft caramel color. It was about a foot long and maybe eight or ten inches high. "He was from Egypt, you know." I said yes, she'd told me. "I want this camel. This is all I'm taking. Just to remember him by." I helped her tuck it down into her cart, and then we said goodbye in front of the building, and she hailed a cab to go home.

I'm not sure why Lois kept only the camel in the end, but I can speak from my own experience: sometimes you hold on to a big thing, an overwhelming thing, because you believe that if you let it go, you'll lose the memories tucked into its walls, its boxes, its cushions and seams. You can't see the way out from under it, and so you ignore the idea of parting with it and let it bend and break even further. What if you let the thing go and you lose a piece of the person who left it to you? Then circumstances tip, or you get a push, and you gather the courage to do it, and it's easier than you anticipate. You hang on to something small. You tuck a camel in a rolling cart, some fabric scraps in a garbage bag, and you promise to find a place for it. You keep what you can carry, and you make it enough.

The next day, at the closing, Lois was the one who was early. We found her sitting at the conference table in a zebra-striped coat and a beret. Before we signed the paperwork, she handed me a MAC Cosmetics bag with a colorful, foldout fan inside. "So you don't forget me!" she said. I wanted to say how impossible that would be, how I would tell the story of this unbelievable apartment for the rest of my life, how indebted I felt to her for giving us the opportunity to live in it, how much I hoped that she would now feel free and unburdened. I wanted to tell her I was worried that if something happened to her, we'd never know. I hadn't met her daughter or any other family members. No one had my number or would call me if Lois got sick or, down the road, passed away.

"I'll talk to you soon," I said. "Maybe I'll call you in a couple of weeks."

Honestly, why stop now?

EPILOGUE

As I finish this book, we have owned the apartment for about two months. It is empty. Our contractor had two workmen bag up and clear out the contents over a couple of weeks. It would have been four or six if the apartment didn't happen to be on the first floor of the building, which allowed the men to toss bags out the front window rather than having to load them onto the freight elevator and ride down to street level. I did not visit every day and watch. I was afraid that, as the men pulled items out of closets and file cabinets, I'd find reasons to keep this or that, and we'd never finish. We donated what we could—a movie props company came and took all of the 1950s medical equipment and old television sets; we found a nursing school that wanted the syringes for students to practice with—and kept a few things, like a couple of the rotary phones and two bedside tables. Neighbors in the building began to notice the door open and the bags going out the front window and asked if they could see the place, this apartment that had been a mystery to people in the building for years. Joan from the seventh floor asked if she could take some empty milk crates she saw stacked in the back bedroom. Ellen from the fifth floor found a ceramic rooster. She collected roosters, she said. I liked the idea of pieces of this apartment, which had sat under everyone's noses all this time, dispersing into the homes around us and finding new life, like dandelion seeds.

The workers found a stack of Lois's husband's old passports while clearing out his office. In some, from Egypt, he was young and stern, with a head of dark, wavy hair and bushy brows. In the more recent ones from the US, his hair was white and wild. "I'm sorry I threw out most of your furniture," I whispered to the photos, and then I wrapped them up into a padded envelope and dropped them at Lois's apartment. I've kept my promise to call periodically. The last time we spoke, she spent fifteen minutes telling me which Salvation Army store in the city she prefers for its superior clothing selection and insisting I watch *The Women*, original 1939 version, which she'd seen on TNT the night before and thought I'd enjoy.

You might be wondering what the strangest thing we found in the apartment was, and it's hard to say, beyond what I've already listed. There was a jug of homemade antiseptic, an unopened Epilady hair-removal device, a 1999 letter of introduction from a genital wart treatment center that was opening down the block. Lois's husband was a Coptic Christian, a religious minority in Egypt that is similar in belief to Greek Orthodoxy. Lois told me he wasn't particularly devout, but as we cleaned out the apartment, we kept finding prayer cards, crucifixes, and small gold and silver charms, meant to hang on a necklace or bracelet, with Jesus or Mary on them. They weren't concentrated in one box or drawer. They were everywhere. Even after I had collected a dozen or so icons, most of them smaller than my thumb pad, we'd move a stool or a garbage bag and see another one hiding in the carpet. It became a joke. How many tiny Jesuses would we find today? On one of the last mornings of the cleanout, I stopped by to see the master bedroom completely empty. The workers had bagged up broken light bulbs, small nuts and bolts, every imaginable little thing, and yet there, on the windowsill, was a pewter oval of the Virgin Mary. Then I found a gold cross on the floor by the bathroom hallway. I can't decide if God is trying to remind me that he is with us in the mess of our lives or that I should be thanking him continuously for this stupid good fortune. I hope it's not an indication that the place is haunted by the spirits of dead saints, because my kids have enough trouble falling asleep as it is.

What I know for sure is that this is it. Once we finish renovating and move into this apartment, I am never moving again. I'm serious. I would like to raise my children, live to an age where I may have lost some of my wits but am not yet incontinent—I mean, I will obviously still be peeing my pants, but I'd be thrilled if it went no further—and be carried out the same way as the file cabinets and nonworking fax machines: through the front window. Is that too much to ask? To be able to stay put? So much movement is thrust upon us. Motherhood warps and changes your body and mind in hundreds of ways. Age gives you perspective that makes you rethink your priorities and principles. Outside circumstances push and squeeze you when you least expect it. Sometimes I wrestle with something willingly, and still, once I change my mind or alter my stance, I would like that to be the end. Finito. Lock the settings; I'm not budging anymore. It's too much work.

But life is never static, even for the stubborn among us. Already, I have found myself open to the idea of guinea pigs.

I will say, though, when finalizing the layout for our new kitchen, we discovered a pipe in the wall that could not be relocated. Its existence dictates that the future entrance to the kitchen will be even narrower and more closed off from the rest of the apartment than we originally wanted, and we all know I already wanted my kitchen to basically be in another county. I dare say, in its current layout, it's going to be like a burrow. A clean, quiet burrow, with no island, just for me. I may never come out.

ACKNOWLEDGMENTS

WRITING A BOOK IS, AS EVERYONE SAYS, A SOLITARY ENDEAVOR, but the beginning of this one was more like being part of a three-legged stool. My agent, Kristin van Ogtrop, and editor, Brigitta Nortker, read early chapters, told me when I didn't sound like myself, and steadied me so I could keep going. I'm so proud of what our little trio turned out. Brigitta, thank you for being enthusiastic about my work long before this book. Kristin, you are one of my favorite writers (and texters), in addition to everything else. Lucky me.

Thank you to my wonderful team and cheering squad, who got these words polished and out into the world: Natalie Nyquist, Claire Drake, Sarah Van Cleve, Lisa Beech, and Stephanie Tresner. Thanks to Shea Nolan for tech support.

Most of my friends have heard me tell these stories over and over, and several of them still read the book and offered feedback. Special thanks to my new friend Holly Edwards as well as my oldest, dearest ones, whose lives I lovingly exploit: Vanessa Buch, Murff Galbreath, Blair Geer, and Hallie Wagner. Huge thanks to Merritt and Jim Holmberg for letting us rent their apartment when we sold ours. It has been a beautiful, soft place to land despite its open kitchen. Thank you to the extended family that makes my work possible: Talysha, Carla, and especially Jeanne, who lights up my children's lives.

To every reader who has sent me a DM on Instagram, asked me to coffee while visiting New York City, or stopped me at Target to say hello: I love you. Meeting you is the best part of this job.

The New York Society Library is my home away from home, and I could not write a single coherent paragraph without it. Thank you to the NYSL staff for giving us writers a gorgeous cocoon in the city to do our work.

For the rest of my life, as I plan to be in my new apartment until I die, I will be grateful to Lois (not her real name). Thank you for picking up the phone every time and following your heart. You made it possible for our family to stay in a building and with a community we cherish.

Finally, I can write so openly about my family because of the steady love mine shows me. Thank you to my sister, Holland, for confidently forging your own path and showing me how to do it too. My mother, Libba, would prefer I never write about her but then provides me with so much good material. Mom, thank you for being in my corner, no matter where it is. Julia, James, and Sam, I adore you. Thanks for forgiving me, teaching me, and being excellent dancers. And to Pass, who tells me never to dedicate a book to him: everything is for you, always, and you know it.

ABOUT THE AUTHOR

ELIZABETH PASSARELLA IS THE AUTHOR OF THE ESSAY COLLECTION *Good Apple,* which was named one of the best books of 2021 by *Real Simple* magazine. Her articles and essays have appeared in the *New York Times, The Wall Street Journal, Vogue, Parents, Martha Stewart Weddings, Real Simple,* and *Southern Living.* Elizabeth is originally from Memphis and now lives in Manhattan with her husband and three children.